The Exploration
of the Secret Smile

American University Studies

Series XXIV
American Literature

Vol. 25

PETER LANG
New York • Bern • Frankfurt am Main • Paris

Alice C. Parker

The Exploration
of the Secret Smile

The Language of Art and of Homosexuality in Frank O'Hara's Poetry

PETER LANG
New York • Bern • Frankfurt am Main • Paris

Library of Congress Cataloging-in-Publication Data

Parker, Alice C.
    The exploration of the secret smile : the language of
art and of homosexuality in Frank O'Hara's poetry /
Alice C. Parker.
    p. cm. — (American university studies.
Series XXIV, American literature ; vol. 25)
    Bibliography: p.
    Includes index.
    1. O'Hara, Frank—Criticism and interpretation.
2. O'Hara, Frank—Knowledge—Art.   3. Homosexuality
in literature.   4. Gay men in literature.   5. Art in
literature.   I. Title.   II. Series.
PS3529.H28Z78   1989   811'54—dc20   89-34163
ISBN 0-8204-0958-8   CIP
ISSN 0895-0512

Edmund Keeley and Philip Sherrard, trans., *C. P. Cavafy:
Collected Poems*, ed. George Savidis. Copyright © 1975
by Edmund Keeley and Philip Sherrard. Selected poems
reprinted with permission of Princeton University Press.

"On Seeing Larry Rivers' *Washington Crossing the
Delaware* at the Museum of Modern Art" From
Meditations in an Emergency. Copyright © 1957 by
Frank O'Hara. Used by permission of Grove Press, a
division of Wheatland Corporation.

Selections reprinted from *The Collected Poems of Frank
O'Hara,* by permission of Alfred A. Knopf, Inc.

"A Step Away from Them" copyright © 1964. Reprinted
by permission of City Lights Books.

CIP-Titelaufnahme der Deutschen Bibliothek

Parker, Alice C.:
    The exploration of the secret smile : the language
of art and of homosexuality in Frank O'Hara's
poetry / Alice C. Parker. – New York; Bern;
Frankfurt am Main; Paris: Lang, 1989.
    (American University Studies: Ser. 24, Ameri-
can Literature; Vol. 25)
    ISBN 0-8204-0958-8

NE: American University Studies / 24

© Peter Lang Publishing, Inc., New York 1989

Printed by Weihert-Druck GmbH, Darmstadt, West Germany

In memory of Alexander Smith, Jr.

THE EXPLORATION OF THE SECRET SMILE: THE
LANGUAGE OF ART AND OF HOMOSEXUALITY IN FRANK
O'HARA'S POETRY

by Alice C. Parker

TABLE OF CONTENTS

CHAPTER I

INTRODUCTION

With relatively few exceptions, and until fairly recently, Frank O'Hara, the poet, has been less seriously regarded than has Frank O'Hara, the highly visible member of a coterie of New York artists and poets in the 1950s and mid-1960s. When O'Hara *has* been considered solely as a poet, the legend of his prolific and casual creativity, his use of a sophisticated city vernacular, and his seemingly "chatty" tone have led some of his critics, particularly the earlier critics and notably the academic and tradition-oriented commentators, to dismiss him as being simply a "light" poet. Later critics have variously attempted to classify O'Hara as a late modernist, or a revolutionary in reaction against high modernism. Many of these latter efforts have been made by other poets, and by critics who are admirers of O'Hara's work, in a certainly justifiable attempt to "legitimize" O'Hara's canon so that it might be permitted a respected place in the mainstream of American poetry.

On the other hand, given the extent of O'Hara's poetic output, detailed criticism of his work has been relatively scant. Moreover, much of the criticism discusses biographical elements which, while constantly present in his poetry, are of peripheral rather than of central concern to the study of the corpus of his work. In addition, there is a small body of writing relating to O'Hara's work in drama and prose, to his collaboration with several visual artists and musicians, to his writing in the art chronicles, and to the memory of Frank O'Hara, a central figure in the world of visual artists and poets in New York in the 1950s and early 1960s.[1]

Fuller studies that are concerned specifically with Frank O'Hara as a poet accept as a given the premise that O'Hara is a poet of the city, and one of the so-called New York poets who admired and were stimulated by the work and aesthetics of the Abstract Expressionist painters. This generally accepted premise, however, is the only fundamental agreement that appears in the criticism concerned with O'Hara's poetic canon.

The two book-length commentaries on Frank O'Hara, Marjorie Perloff's *Poet Among Painters*, and Alan Feldman's *Frank O'Hara*, both discuss, from obviously separate perspectives, the multi-faceted involvement that O'Hara maintained in the world of the New York poets, and in the New York art world. Perloff's, the longer and more detailed of the two works, treats O'Hara's poetry chronologically, and while she tells us that her focus is critical rather than biographical, the effectiveness of her discourse leans heavily on facts of O'Hara's life. His poetry is so decidedly autobiographical, however, that it would be impossible for any critical interpretation of that poetry to ignore, completely, biographical facts. Perloff stresses that, as opposed to a still persistent critical bias, O'Hara was a serious and "highly sophicated poet with strong tastes of his own," and that he "debunks the 'beautiful' and elevates the obscene to poetic status."[2] *Poet Among Painters* clearly indicates that Perloff considers O'Hara to be a poet who made a major contribution to American poetry in the 1950s and early 1960s.

Alan Feldman likewise deals with various aspects of O'Hara's life in relation to his poetry, and he also analyzes, separately, certain observed qualities that inhere in the poems, particularly the emotional content and the humor. He calls O'Hara's emotional authenticity "one of his works's most important qualities, . . ." and says of his humor that he uses it "to subvert conventional values."[3] Feldman, of course, acknowledges O'Hara as a "city" poet, and predicts that "no American poet of city life will escape some debt to O'Hara in the future."[4] Despite the length of these two works, and the precise analysis of a number of O'Hara's poems contained in each of them, the reader is left with a sense of doubt concerning the authors' definitive assessments of O'Hara's achievement, purely as a poet.

This sense of doubt seems not to permeate the shorter commentaries on O'Hara's poetry. On the one hand, there are a few critics who either dismiss O'Hara as being a "gifted writer determined to be trivial, . . ."[5] or who say variously of his poetry: "Light and chatty, his often seem to be anti-poems, the product of a pop-camp imagination, . . ."[6] that it belongs in the American tradition of "personal poetry" that extends back through Williams to Whitman,[7] or who, in an effort to be all-inclusive, call O'Hara "a poet-curator-critic."[8]

There are, on the other hand, those critics who address specific qualities in O'Hara's poetry, and who analyze those qualities from a particular aesthetic perspective. Then there are others, many of whom are poets themselves, who are admittedly partisan, favoring O'Hara's poetry for a variety of reasons that range through the spectrum of the aesthetics of poetry.

Helen Vendler, in *Part of Nature, Part of Us*, falls somewhere between both categories. She addresses the question of form, or lack of it, in the poems, and concludes that while O'Hara himself was not troubled by the question, his work was marred by a "lack of comfortable form . . ." as well as by "a radical incapacity for abstraction. . . ."[9] Yet, she admires O'Hara's "simplicity" and his "integrity cherishing the variety of the self and the world. . . ." And, because of his "fine multiplicity" and his absence of "intellectual syntax," she says he is a "poet to be reckoned with, a new species."[10]

This seems, indeed, to be faint praise from Vendler. Writing in 1980, she is obviously persuaded that O'Hara is, as she says, "to be reckoned with," but the vagueness of her commentary suggests that she is not thoroughly convinced about why that may be so. Donald Hall may have thrown a bit of light on this sense of vagueness recently, when he stated in an interview: "*The New Yorker*, by appointing Helen Vendler, resigned from reviewing poetry. . . . She can write a sentence, but she has no *taste*. She's a bobby-soxer for poets she croons over: some good, some bad, she can't tell the difference. . . ."[11]

Susan Holohan also cites O'Hara's innovative syntax and "his remarkable way of making a sentence, or not making a sentence . . ." and links it to his immediate appreciation of the present moment.[12]

This appreciation of the present moment is also commented upon by his friend and fellow "New York poet," James Schyler in an interview for *The American Poetry Review* in 1985. Schyler was asked: "Would you compare yourself to Frank O'Hara?" and his response was a telling one with regard to both a poet's natural antipathy to being compared with another poet, and to his assessment of one aspect of O'Hara's work. He said: "I don't think I write like he did. Well, I think Frank's poems are often more like diary entries than mine are."[13]

The present moment, from another critical stance, is addressed by Thomas Meyer in a review of Perloff's *Poet Among Painters*, and of O'Hara's *Early Writing* and *Poems Retrieved*. Meyer comments on the poet's "valid desire to create a new surface . . .,"[14] and this comment, based on an aesthetic metaphor, reflects a sense of the immediacy that is in O'Hara's poetry. We do indeed get a strong sense of O'Hara's "new surface"—"his immediacy"—as it is revealed in his poetic re-creation of the present moment, and in his clear recognition that the creating of the poem *about* the immediate moment is a component *of* the reality of that moment.

This "immediacy" is again noted in Anthony Libby's comparison of O'Hara's poetic sense of the moment with Jackson Pollock's spon-taneous "drip" paintings. Libby points out that "much of O'Hara is no more matter-of-fact or trivial than Pollock. Behind the trivia there is a magic radiance, however elusive. . . ."[15] Jackson Pollock, the Action Painter and an integral part of the New York group of artists before his untimely death, was extremely involved with "surface" and "line" in his innovative canvasses. Libby compares the immediacy of Pollock's visual "lines" to that of O'Hara's poetic lines, saying that they both depend upon an "apparently unselfconscious tension between free-dom of gesture and instinctive control. . . ."[16] And, as we shall see below,

O'Hara himself, in "Digressions on *Number 1*, 1948," speaks of the relation between his "lines" and Pollock's, and of his admiration for the painter's "perfect hand."

The element of tension is discussed also by Charles Altieri in *Enlarging the Temple*, a work directed to the discussion of the aesthetic of presence in the postmodern poetry of the 1960s. In the chapter, "Varieties of Immanentist Experience: Robert Bly, Charles Olson, and Frank O'Hara," Altieri says of O'Hara's poetry: "as soon as one requires specific personal and secular meanings from this poetic, he finds himself tormented by pressures to have each moment of experience provide in intensity what it cannot give on the level of ideas or principles."[17] Altieri also calls O'Hara the poet of "the domestic and the quotidian."[18]

Paul Carroll, one of the first critical commentators to note the importance of O'Hara's poetry, also points to tension, and to the lack of it, as well as to what Altieri calls "the domestic and the quotidian." In "An Impure Poem About July 17, 1959,"[19] Carroll discusses O'Hara's well-known poem, "The Day Lady Died," with reference to the New Critical precept of "organicism" and the tenet that a poem should fully develop its potential significance. He points out that O'Hara shows, in other works, that he can, indeed, write an "organic" poem, but that in "Lady," he does not develop the significance of the early and ironic reference to Bastille Day, and that the poem is filled with seemingly trivial and irrelevant details. Carroll makes no reference here to Robert Penn Warren's earlier essay, "Impure Poetry," in which Warren says: "nothing that is available in human experience is to be legislated out of poetry, . . ."[20] but Carroll, in essence, agrees with its premise. He says that "Lady" is "excellent *because* of its trivia, . . ." also, that it contains no "tension," and that it is one of the first, and remains one of the finest, examples of "impure poetry." Carroll feels that anything can exist in a poem, and "in whatever way the poet chooses."[21] Charles Molesworth carries this idea further when he says that "O'Hara wanted his poems to assume the status of things, and he was even willing to run the risk that they would sink to the level of commodities. . . ." He sums up this assessment by judging O'Hara's poetry to be "completely American."[22]

With regard to some of the more partisan critics—those who, in essence, know O'Hara's poetry best—such as Kenneth Koch, Bill Berkson, John Ashbery, and O'Hara's editor, Donald Allen—there is agreement on a number of issues, but no genuine consensus on the virtues of that poetry. Koch calls O'Hara "consistently experimental,"[23] Ashbery, in *In Memory of My Feelings,* is quoted as referring to him as "an animateur," and Berkson says that he was always "conscious of artists other than himself."[24] Donald Allen says of O'Hara and of the other poets included in *The New American Poetry,* that they had one common characteristic: "a total rejection of all those qualities typical of academic verse. . . ." He also notes that much of the poetry was closely allied to Abstract Expressionist painting.[25] O'Hara's acquaintance with the works of the Abstract Expressionists, his interaction with them, and his admiration of their work is attested to by the poems in his canon that either directly or indirectly address their similar aesthetic concerns. We shall examine some of these commonalities in the following chapter.

John Ashbery, in his Introduction to *The Collected Poems of Frank O'Hara,* expands on Allen's point-of-view. He says that O'Hara's poems ignored the rules for modern American poetry from Pound and Eliot to the academic establishments of the 1940s, and that his early work "was met with the friendly silence reserved for the thoroughly unacceptable guest." Ashbery also tells us that the use of the vernacular, the autobiographical element, the "space" of New York City, as well as a quality of "openness," identify O'Hara's poetics. "[T]he work seems entirely natural and available to the multitude of big and little phenomena which combine to make that almost unknowable substance that is our experience. This openness is the essence of Frank

O'Hara's poetry, and it is why he is read by increasing numbers of those who, in Kenneth Koch's phrase, are 'dying for the truth.'"[26] The "truth," however, does not seem to include, for Koch, Ashbery, et al., the truth of the homosexual element in his poetry, since they never allude to it. It seems appropriate to question here then, why that important aspect of O'Hara's poetry was not addressed by his friends and fellow poets. Perhaps one obvious conclusion that we might draw from this lacuna is that the topic, or subject, in any of its forms, would no doubt have impeded the desired "legitimizing" of O'Hara's poetry, and so it was deliberately avoided in their commentary.

And yet, "openness" in the sense that it is used above, is indeed a highly visible quality in O'Hara's poetry. Openness of form, of syntax, of thought pattern, and openness to an innovative use of subject matter are apparent throughout his work. The critical view then, that O'Hara is "trivial," and a "light" poet, and that his poetry suffers from lack of form does not seem to be a view that can be supported by a close examination of his work. O'Hara experiments with form throughout his canon: his poetry varies from page to page and from poem to poem in the form he creates to suit his content, as well as in the traditional forms that he chooses to use, or to alter, or to ignore. And because of his inclusiveness concerning his experience and the details encompassing it as valid subject matter for his poetry, it is not impossible to mis-translate the inclusion of witty, or chatty, or trivial details in the poem into O'Hara as a poet of the "trivial." But he indeed often does *deliberately* "trivialize" as a form of meiosis, and he *is*, truly, the poet of the "domestic and the quotidian."

In this connection, while Cleanth Brooks wrote the following in 1935, and while he was referring to the "radical poetry of the *moderns*" (emphasis mine), the point he makes concerning Matthew Arnold's phrase "high seriousness" might easily be applied to the early critical reception accorded to O'Hara's poetry, and to that of other New York poets, in the late 1950s and early 1960s:

> For seventy-five years Arnold's phrase has defined the inner sanctum of poetry, effectually excluding from it those spurious poetries, *vers de société*, satire and all the other varieties, either flippant or bitter or trifling, of the poetry of wit. The necessity for high seriousness . . . is usually the principle appealed to in order to discredit the radical poetry of the moderns. It is convenient in that although it allows the critic to compliment such poets for their cleverness, it makes it possible for him to deny that they are true poets at all.[27]

We turn now to a very different critical perspective. In "Gay Language as Political Praxis," Bruce Boone traces many of the above noted and other critical commentaries that attempt to place O'Hara in one or another theoretical or aesthetic poetic position, and states that O'Hara's poetry has now become "legitimate." But, he points out, these legitimizing efforts result in repressing the sexual content of O'Hara's poetry, as well as in repressing the "antagonistic sexual language in the poems." Boone discusses an element of O'Hara's poetic style that makes use of the language of an "alternative" group in New York City, that of the gay community.[28]

The homosexual sub-culture also informed much of the subject matter celebrated in O'Hara's poetry. The recognition of his deliberate use of that subject matter and of the language practice of the gay world at a time when that language was actually available only to the members of the gay community is of vital importance to any understanding of his poetic, and to locating a mutality of milieu for that poetic.

Similarly, O'Hara's immersion in the volatile art world of New York City in the 1950s and early 1960s, and his attendant peripatetic daily involvement with Abstract Expressionist and Action painters, gives evidence of his aesthetic involvement with their notions of the appropriate form and subject matter of contemporary art. His aesthetic involvement, as well as his perceptions as a member of the New York homosexual community, inform a significant part of O'Hara's poetic canon and they will be the main focus of concern in this essay.

In the 1950s and early 1960s, New York was the center of artistic activity for a group of non-objective painters who became known as Abstract Expressionists, and for a number of poets who found the aesthetics of Abstract Expressionism extremely congenial to their own art. In the light of critical attention, it was the visual artists who claimed the most notice, but the poets, with O'Hara central among them, comprised a viable, if not especially cohesive, literary counterpart. O'Hara's centrality was due, on one hand, of course, to his direct professional involvement with the Museum of Modern Art. (He worked at the Museum from 1951 to 1953, when he left to become an editorial associate for *Art News*. O'Hara rejoined the Museum as special assistant in the International Program in 1955, and was appointed Associate Curator in 1965.) But on the other hand, and more impor- tantly to the present purpose, his centrality was due to his intense creativity and dedication as a poet.

Along with O'Hara, poets such as James Schyler, Kenneth Koch, John Ashbery,[29] Bill Berkson, and Edwin Denby found New York to be a fulcrum, "a city where they met and continued their lives together. . . ."[30] But it is O'Hara, Koch, and Ashbery who "form the fountain of influences"[31] in what has been referred to as the New York School. These New York poets, however, despite their shared involvement in the artistic ambience of the city, did not share a general poetic aesthetic. What they did share, and what O'Hara's poetry clearly indicates, was a rejection of "the formalism, conservatism and 'classicism' of Eliot's influence on American writing, . . ." and a kinship with William Carlos Williams' "new poetics."[32]

As John Bernard Myers describes these poets in his Introduction to *The Poets of the New York School*, they were "a group of writers rejected by the literary establishment who found strength to continue with their work by what the anarchists used to call 'mutual aid.'"[33] But these poets were united by more than simply the rejection of the literary establishment (which has been the fate of most poets throughout literary history who have taken a different poetic path from that of their immediate forebears).

The positive artistic connection among all of the New York poets was that they shared a "basic attitude of directness and spontaneity in their work, all have in one way or another broken with tradition and investigated new approaches to their art, and have broken down the division between art and life."[34]

It is clear that the positive effects of the stimuli of the city on their work was a quality that united all of these poets. And O'Hara, in his work at the Museum of Modern Art, in addition to his own poetic productivity, was one of the creators of the stimuli, as well as being one of those who were stimulated. Kenneth Koch, in 1961, writing about O'Hara's controversial *Second Avenue*, remarked that "Mr. O'Hara is the best writer about New York alive . . . he succeeds in conveying the city's atmosphere not by writing directly about it but by writing about his emotions, all of them somehow filtered through its paint supply stores and its inspiring April smog."[35] Yet Koch also tells us in an interview in 1982, that "[O'Hara] seems to have been inspired by everything that was full of life, energy, excitement, and force. But, no, it wasn't just painting."[36]

If O'Hara were not the "best" poet writing about New York at the time, it can at least be said with certainty that he was one of the most intensely involved New York poets, in addition to being one of the most positively partisan.

Clearly then, the locus of O'Hara's poetry is the city—his centrality is New York City—and if we can be certain about any aspect of his poetry, albeit with only a negative certainty, it is that O'Hara is not a pastoral poet:[37]

However, I have never clogged myself with the praises of
   pastoral life, nor
with nostalgia for an innocent past of perverted acts in
   pastures. No. One need
never leave the confines of New York to get all the
   greenery one wishes—I
can't even enjoy a blade of grass unless I know there's
   a subway handy, or a
record store or some other sign that people do not
   totally *regret* life.

                    ("Meditations in an Emergency," *CP*, p. 197)

In the contemporary world, O'Hara is not alone in such a perception. But the unquestioning embrace that O'Hara gives to what might be called the city's "teeming isolation" in the middle of the 20th century, is not at one with the reactions of earlier poets of the late 18th and early 19th centuries, to the complexity of the growing metropolis, when the modern city first became the locus of poetry. At that time, the early, traditional view of innocence-in-the country-and-vice-in-the-city no longer held, and it was gradually replaced by a tone of concerned ambivalence. To Blake, the "innocence and vice were in and of the city. . . ." In his poem, "London," he sees "Marks of weakness, marks of woe . . ." in every face. There was a new way of seeing men in a new kind of city. Innocence had become a victim of the "mind-forg'd manacles . . ." of repression inflicted by a changing society.

Wordsworth, in "Residence in London," the seventh book of *The Prelude*, is in awe of the vast metropolis, but sees also that love does not thrive there. He senses a "strangeness, a loss of connection . . . a failure of identity. . . ." This early sense of alienation is echoed in the late 19th century. In *The City of Dreadful Night*, and *The Doom of a City*, by James Thomson, and in the late novels of Thomas Hardy, there is a mourning for a societal loss of community. The isolation and separation and danger that these authors saw in the city can be traced into the 20th century to the "city of death in life," the modern wasteland of Eliot.[38]

Yet the city, during the 19th and into the early 20th century, was also a generative source for the artist, as well as a center of intellectual life. In essence, there has always been, historically, a close association between literature and cities. The exponents of modernism, in fact, insist that the "quest for self and art alike can only be carried out in the glare and existential posture of the city. . . ."[39]

But, while O'Hara carried out his "quest" in New York City, his was not a "quest for self and art," but rather a quest for "being" and "experiencing." And, simultaneously, he sought to explore the actual writing of his poetry concerning this "experiencing." Again unlike the modernists, O'Hara did not feel himself to be an exile in the city, nor did he look upon the city itself as a "wasteland" that would have to be brought to renewal by some transcending human force. The classic defensive pose of the modernists concerning their concept that the city has no objective reality, and their on-going debate with an "imagined interlocutor" concerning that concept,[40] is foreign to "O'Hara's ready acceptance of the milieu of the city. This is not to say, however, that he did not "see" or feel the alienation of man from man, and of man from his environment, that exists in the city. He saw it clearly, accepted it as the necessary condition of modern-day inhabitants of the city, and made it an integral concept of his poetry.

But while O'Hara did indeed have an imaginary "interlocutor" in many, or perhaps in most, of his poems, there was no "debate" between the two concerning the city's lack of objective reality. Rather, there was a "shared monologue" in which O'Hara explored his sense of the city, and what it contained as a source of creativity, of visual stimuli, and of imaginative expansion. From this rich and complex mother-lode he mined among other things, a seemingly inexhaustible supply of highly original (and to many of his critics, highly controversial) poetic subject matter.

In essence, the reality of the city for O'Hara existed in its continuous production of engaging and stimulating details.[41] The multitudinous phenomena that assault one's consciousness in the city constantly transpose, shift, and metamorphose. Consequently, the meanings of those phenomena are, likewise, perpetually changing. O'Hara's poetic tone, therefore, takes on the texture of urban ca-caphony in a seemingly patternless sifting of momentary experience. A pattern, however, does emerge in the poetry he creates from within this helter-skelter environment, and it is stitched together by O'Hara's deliberate involvement with minute details.

This involvement is expressed in a poetic language that is stripped of any conscious reliance on accepted syntax and is, instead, a sometimes frustrating augmentation of the frenetic motion of city life. His use of parataxis and asyndeton is also, in many instances, his immediate response to the welter of simultaneous stimuli coming from his environment, and is a means of re-creating that simultaneity in his poems. Other contemporary writers, such as Lowell and Berryman, also omit connectives in some of their verse, but in their work it seems to be more a conscious use of rhetorical device rather than as in O'Hara's case, a natural response to the pace of the city.

In addition, his frequent use of an asyntactic style is also a reflection of city pace and adds a sense of "fragmentation" to his poetry. But the use of that style has another purpose, and a further result. It can be perceived as a private means of expressing the experiences of the alternative life-style of the gay community in New York City with which he was directly involved; a close reading of O'Hara's poetry from this perspective rewards one with a hitherto unsuspected view of that life-style.

A useful overview of O'Hara's concern with the city is provided by O'Hara himself, and is quoted in Bill Berkson's Afterword to *In Memory of My Feelings.* In a monologue that O'Hara wrote for the Abstract Expressionist painter, Franz Kline, "Franz Kline Talking," O'Hara has Kline say:

> Hell, half the world wants to be like Thoreau at Walden worrying about the noise on the way to Boston; the other half use up their lives being part of that noise. I like the second half. Right? . . .
>
> ("Afterword," p. 1)

And Hugh Kenner's description of New York City might also function as an encompassing metaphor for O'Hara's consuming interest in the city:

> . . . a visitor to New York City at any time is apt to feel that the place is in process of being improvised. Structures run up, abandoned, left behind in a night; graffiti; sound and light shows, irridescences; neon; footnotes to history; registrations of the current, persistences in the memory. . . .[42]

Indeed, the final sentence above could stand as an impressionistic overview of Frank O'Hara's stylistic approach to the creation of his poetry in the locus of New York.

It is pertinent here, then, to consider briefly O'Hara's stated poetic theories, and their relation to the creation of that poetry. The discussion of those theories will necessarily be brief, since he gave short shrift to his own theoretical conjectures, as well as to the theoretical poetic formulations of other poets. This is not to say that he treated them with any lack of due respect; rather, he had more faith in the experience of writing the poem than in the theorizing about writing it.

In "Personism: A Manifesto," first published in *Yugen*, in 1961,[43] O'Hara says that he is absolutely opposed to the "abstract removal" of the poet from his poetry. The "person" in "Personism" is the omnipresent other who is addressed by the poet, the imaginary "interlocutor" mentioned previously, the "other" (and often the other "self") with whom the poet is directly communicating. The emphasis on the personal and on the moment is the hallmark of O'Hara's poetics, but as is often the case with poets, that emphasis is perceived more readily in his poetry than in his theoretical statements. As an example, he tells us in "Personism" that measure and other "technical apparatus" are "just common sense: if you're going to buy a pair of pants you want them to be tight enough so that everyone will want to go to bed with you." His comparison here seems somewhat removed from the poetic under discussion, but the actual form of his poems does derive from "common sense," in the purport of the early modernist architectural dictum that "form follows function." In his odes he typically uses a relatively "nobler" diction and a more formal structure; in his love poems a tight lyric form. In a polemical poem, as in "Agression" (CP, pp. 263-64), a poem concerned with both sexual and military agression, the first line of every stanza is projected five or six spaces (depending on the use of upper or lower case letters) to the left, so that it becomes virtually a visual prod. The nine stanzas of the poem thereby present the appearance of military precision, which displays the verbal content of the poem in visual form. In other instances, a number of O'Hara's poems seem simply to range across the printed page with an almost arbitrarily defined lineation. But, true to O'Hara's emphasis on the immediate, this implies that: "This among other things simply happened—a form which subsumes structure and event into active meaning."[44]

In his statement for *The New American Poetry: 1945-1960*, O'Hara says that he doesn't feel that his experiences are "clarified" or "made beautiful" for himself or for anyone else; they are just "there."

16

"What is clear to me in my work is probably obscure to others and vice versa. My formal stance is found at the crossroads where what I know and can't get meets what is left of what I know and can bear without hatred" (*CP*, p. 500). This concept is exemplified and even made poignantly clear in the short poem, "At Joan's":

> It is almost three
> I sit at the marble top
> sorting poems, miserable
> the little lamp glows feebly
> I don't glow at all
>
> I have another cognac
> and stare at two little paintings
> of Jean-Paul's, so great
> I must do so much
> or did they just happen
>
> the breeze is cool
> barely a sound filters up
> through my confused eyes
> I am lonely for myself
> I can't find a real poem
> if it won't happen to me
> what shall I do
> (*CP*, pp. 327-28)

O'Hara's experience, here the poet's anguish at the tyranny of the blank page, *is* the poem, and as he has said, it is just "there." But despite the apparent casualness of his "poetics," the poem suggests that art—both his and others'—is of crucial importance to him, and he

insists elsewhere on the "seriousness" of his art. In a short poem called
"The Critic," written in 1951, he says:

> I cannot possibly think of you
> other than you are: the assassin
>
> of my orchards. You lurk there
> in the shadows, meting out
>
> conversation like Eve's first
> confusion between penises and
>
> snakes. Oh be droll, be jolly
> and be temperate! Do not
>
> frighten me more than you
> have to! I must live forever.
> (CP, p. 48)

As is apparent above, O'Hara's "openness" and his tendency
toward the autobiographical are two active qualities that inform all of
his poetry, and they are reflected upon as well in his brief references
to his poetics. His eye for detail and his inclusiveness follow from these
qualities, but while he does not dwell on these activating principles in
his prose commentary, they nonetheless contribute to the sense of
existential tension that his poetry reflects.

But tension in O'Hara's poetry, as well as in his poetic theories,
is not expressed as personal dismay, or despair, or individual alienation. His poetry actually celebrates the activity—the motion and
commotion—of life while simultaneously inscribing into the poetic text
the underlying potential for psychological destruction. This dialectic
between presence and alienation contributes to his own sense of poetic

equilibrium, and this equilibrium is actually the sense of significance that he apprehends in the urban milieu. ("Presence, in O'Hara's poetry, is simply the recovery of familiar aspects of urban contemporary life, aspects whose value resides not in the deeper forces they reveal, but rather in the qualities of emotional expression or of wit they elicit.") Like urban life itself, O'Hara can depend upon "only the unity of mad process"[45] for coherence in the perpetual activity expressed in his poems.

As truncated and summary as are his poetic statements, O'Hara makes his primary poetic objective quite clear: the actual experience of writing the poem is the basis for his poetics; his emphasis is on performance.[46] The basic ingredients of O'Hara's poetry are experiences; *his* experiences, and his simultaneous perceptions of them as he writes the poem that contains them. These perceptions are also "immediate" because he provides minute details in what seems to be everyday language, so that the communication becomes as real, in a performative sense, as are the experiences themselves. "To 'do' one's art means to solve problems in a language which the art establishes as it is being created. Its grammar and lexicon emerge less as a result of a commitment to prior forms and more as a response to immediate necessity."[47]

"Presence" as well as "performance" are hallmarks of O'Hara's poetry, and while his influence on other poets is for the most part as yet undocumented, it is attested to in various quarters. His materials are as important as are his attitudes to that influence, "as indications of areas in human experience not often mined by poets." His attitudes are influential particularly on those taken by his humility and skepticism. "One so aware of the arbitrary creativity he requires to make the present vital is not apt to take either himself, or his poetry, or his world view as possible salvation for everyone."[48] In *The Poets of the New York School*, John Bernard Myers calls O'Hara "perhaps the most typical of the 'unofficial poets,'" and says that "he encouraged in one way or another" New York poets such as Ashbery, Koch, Schyler, Guest, Elmslie, Lima, Ceravolo, and Towle.[49]

While O'Hara's premature death precluded his participation in the current oral poetry movement, surely his sense of the "present" and his sense of "immediacy," as exhibited in his poetry and as stated in "Personism"—"While I was writing it [a poem for a lover] I was realizing that if I wanted to I could use the telephone instead of writing the poem . . ."[50]—places him in the vanguard of influence on performative poetry. Since the late sixties, oral poetry, "defined for the most part by its tendency to regard poetry as an oral, performance-oriented medium rather than as a written and text-oriented object, has been slowly transforming American poetics." This poetic movement, however, faces, in academic circles, the "instant panic and revulsion" that was the plight of "that earlier fifties avant-garde"—Beat, Black Mountain, and New York poets. Oral poetry then, its "sense of the present a 'sense of urgency,'"[51] is perhaps another aspect of American poetry upon which O'Hara's poetic innovativeness has had and will have an important influence.[52]

But even though O'Hara's poetic practice emphasizes "performance" and "presence," his thematic concerns are somewhat reminiscent of those of the earlier modernist and high modernist poets. The poetry of Eliot, Robinson, Crane, Williams, among others, expresses the concerns of death of the spirit and death of nature, the prospect of death and rebirth, the value of acceptance, and, specifically, the despair and alienation found in the city, despite its continuous and often alluring excitement and activity. O'Hara expresses concern regarding the dual notion of death, the multiple possibilities of "death" aligned with "rebirth," and he accepts the despair and alienation found in the city, as well as the exciting activity that is ever-present there. To him it is a place of activity and pleasure and fun and artistic and sexual activity. The attendant pain and suffering must be avoided or overcome, however, and O'Hara overcomes them with a good deal of irony and resolve. Among other things, his poetry reflects a systematic resistance to self-importance and sentimentality. And that resistance is conducted by embracing the *seemingly* trivial—including the triviality of the self—by almost willing himself to be content with the quotidian, in whatever form it appears, rather than by yearning for the cosmic.

O'Hara's thematic concerns, but particularly his language, are reminiscent also of those of Whitman. Mutlu Konuk Blasing, in her *American Poetry: The Rhetoric of Its Forms*, suggests that Whitman's strategy, as well as O'Hara's, is anagogic; "a coincidence of textual and existential experience, figurative and literal language, poetic and natural form." She points out that "[b]reaking down the distinction between form and content these poets use the collage method and epic forms, in which disorder and order, accident and design, multiplicity and unity, formlessness and form, a quantitive 'all' and a qualitative 'All' coincide." She tells us, too, that O'Hara's place in the Whitmanic tradition has not yet been sorted out, but that he "resusitates the Whitmanic breath with greater success than any of his contemporaries." And, O'Hara continues as well, in the Romantic tradition that alligns art and nature.[53]

To O'Hara, however, "nature" means *human* nature, and often includes a particular emphasis on *homosexual* nature, against the destructiveness of materialism. Bruce Boone's assessment then, that the main body of criticism of O'Hara's work ignores, and so represses, the homosexual content of the poetry, is a valid assessment, and is of the first importance in this discussion of O'Hara's poetry.

Frank O'Hara was an intensely serious New York poet who used innovative diction, syntax, and subject matter to form a poetic canon that re-creates his myriad atypical and typical experiences into a viable and noteworthy poetic achievement. Through his use of these innovative means, through his obvious empathy with Whitmanian poetics and concerns, through his knowledge of the Abstract Expressionists and of their art, and through his knowledge of the New York (and extended) homosexual community, O'Hara's achieved effect is one of spontaneity, simultaneity, antinomy of intensity and detachment, and, in his use of what has been called "oppositional"[54] language, one that re-creates an intimate, personal view of the dynamics of a particular segment of New York City life. Far from being merely chatty, "chic," gossipy, trivial, sophisticatedly obscure, or being only a *reflection* of Abstract Expressionist aesthetics in poetry, much of O'Hara's canon is a concrete manifestation of his conscious, deliberate, intense, and continuous creative involvement with even the most minute details of his daily experience in the worlds of art and homosexuality. And his creative involvement, like Whitman's, is augmented by his poetic stance oblique from the periphery.

The homosexual content of O'Hara's poetry is, in essence, one of the two converging lines of O'Hara's poetic perspective to be examined below. The other is his poetic use of the language of the visual arts. The gist of this essay, then, is that there can be a critical reading of O'Hara's poetry of New York that supplements the one that "legitimized" his poetry; a reading that emphasizes the frequent fusion of the aesthetics of poetry with the aesthetics of the visual arts, and that particularly emphasizes a private and largely over-looked aspect of O'Hara's work: the aspect of the urban homosexual, or gay, experience. This reading reveals the importance of the deliberately (given the societal "mood" of the '50s and '60s) sedimented homosexual meaning in O'Hara's poetry, and of the importance of his use of the language of the visual arts, to the full realization of the vitality and congruence of his poetic canon.

CHAPTER II

THE PERFORMANCE OF THE VISUAL

In O'Hara's poem, "Radio," his involvement in the world of the visual arts is clearly in evidence. Here, his daily involvement in that world is explicit, as is, in the final lines of the poem, his poetic involvement with the aesthetics of painting.

> Why do you play such dreary music
> on Saturday afternoon, when tired
> mortally tired I long for a little
> reminder of immortal energy?
>   All
> week long while I trudge fatiguingly
> from desk to desk in the museum
> you spill your miracles of Grieg
> and Honegger on shut-ins.
>   Am I not
> shut in too, and after a week
> of work don't I deserve Prokofieff?
>
> Well, I have my beautiful de Kooning
> to aspire to. I think it has an orange
> bed in it, more than the ear can hold.
>   (CP, p. 234)

As we see in these lines, O'Hara uses the horizontal correspondences of synaesthesia to mark the simultaneity of his aesthetic perceptions:

> Well, I have my beautiful de Kooning
> to aspire to. I think it has an orange
> bed in it, more than the ear can hold.

He does this often and casually in his poetry, as, for example, in the first few lines of "A Step Away From Them," when he refers to "hum-colored cabs," and, as we saw in "At Joan's," when he says: "barely a sound filters up / through my confused eyes." This sort of rhetorical reference, of course, seems quite natural in poems that recreate his day-to-day existence in the cosmopolitan, never-sleeping, constantly-moving environment of a very large city.

O'Hara's use of synaesthesia here is reminiscent of the poetry of Baudelaire, and particularly of Baudelaire's famous "Correspondances," from *Les Fleurs du Mal*. Both Baudelaire and O'Hara were art critics as well as poets, and the visual, aural, and verbal senses were constantly interacting in their professional, as well as in their physical lives. Both were also considered to have been *les flâneurs*, men-about-town.

Another of O'Hara's poetic precursors, the early French surrealist poet, Apollinaire, was also known for his astute art criticism, especially concerning the Cubists, and was one of O'Hara's "heroes."[1] While O'Hara was self-admittedly influenced by these French poets (and by later ones as Valéry and Reverdy: "My heart is in my / pocket, it is Poems by Pierre Reverdy."),[2] they are of interest here primarily because of the parallel between them and O'Hara in their strong identification, as poets, with the world of the visual arts. As Libby points out, "Frank O'Hara is an unusually conspicuous example of the interaction between American poetry and modern painting."[3]

In his monograph on Jackson Pollock, for instance, O'Hara tells us that art in America "was changed by Surrealism, and even if more literary than painterly works influenced American life, the basic findings of the Surrealist struggle toward subliminal meaning has not failed to effect [sic] all modern art. . . ."[4] With specific reference to Action Painting, and to the concept of "spiritual clarity," O'Hara asks:

But how much clarity can a human being bear? This state may be the ultimate goal of the artist, yet for the man it is most ardous. Only the artist who has reached this state should be indicated by Harold Rosenberg's well-known designation Action Painter, for only when he is in this state is the artist's 'action' significant purely and simply of itself. . . . Action Painting did not emerge miraculously from the void, and it is interesting and even comforting to make not-too-far-fetched analogies with the works of predecessors because art is, after all, the visual treasury of man's world, as well as of individual men.[5]

Although the terms Abstract Expressionism and Action Painting are sometimes used interchangeably, it is useful here to note the difference in emphasis in these two closely related, yet distinct forms of painting. While Abstract Expressionism is a general term used for an "imageless painting, antiformal, improvisatory, energetic and free in its brushwork,"[6] Action Painting specifically involves "splashing and dribbling paint on canvas. The basis assumption is that the Unconscious will take over and produce a work of art."[7] Both forms of painting are obviously derivitive from Surrealism, and expressive of the immediacy of the creative process.

In a literary context, it is clear that O'Hara's poetry, in particular those poems that address the concerns of art and of artists, or that reflect on the visual and the poetic simultaneously, are indicative of these same aesthetic qualities. There is also, in his poetry, the immanentist tendency to allow for the free and automatic self-arrangement of his materials, and an emphasis on performance and play, or "action." There is no traditional hierarchy of syntax, no effort to conceal dichotomy or paradox, and, while in O'Hara perceptions of reality are detailed, there is a lack of concern for the representation of the "real," or the reality of representation. The drawing from the unconscious, the subconscious, and the dream state (as in "Second Avenue," [q.v. *CP*, pp. 139-150]), underlies much of O'Hara's early poetry.

Another and very evident commonality of O'Hara and the Abstract Expressionists, is that both their arts are indigenous to the city: they reflect the qualities of impulse and chance, and there is reflected in them "a deep regard for formal structure while apparently chaotic and indeterminate in appearance. . . ." Their reality is "involved in a constant and never-finished process of movement, development and change."[8]

On the other hand, despite the concurrences and similarities of their aesthetic stance, O'Hara's poetry of that time is not simply a verbal reflection of the canvasses of the New York School of artists. Nor are the emphases on abstraction executed in a similar manner. O'Hara does not remove himself from his poems, as he points out in "Person-ism," as does the Abstract Expressionist painter from his painting (in this O'Hara remains closer to Pollock, who is often literally standing "in" his paintings); he, and his immediate perceptions *are* the poems. He "paints" his perceptions in the language of immediacy and simul-taneity; yet there *is* a kind of "removal," or abstraction, in his poetry. And that "removal" is the poet's immediate and simultaneous move out of an event or scene toward his own perception of it and reaction to its stimuli, and the move back to the actuality of the experience— including the writing of the poem that re-creates it. And O'Hara's poetry records this intellectual/sensual-emotional "push-pull"; out of his complex and potent relationship with the Abstract Expressionist movement, he created the poems that present us with a vital aspect of the aesthetic of his poetry.

It is relevant to look here at "Digressions on *Number 1, 1948*," a poem that reflects on Pollock's painting, *Number 1*, and that addresses itself to the processes and thought patterns behind its creation. At the same time, the poem indicates the connections between the poet's emo-tions and the visual/poetic aesthetic that stimulated them:

I am ill today but I am not
too ill. I am not ill at all.
It is a perfect day, warm
for winter, cold for fall.

A fine day for seeing. I see
ceramics, during lunch hour, by
Miró, and I see the sea by Legér;
light, complicated Metzingers
and a rude awakening by Brauner,
a little table by Picasso, pink.

I am tired today but I am not
too tired. I am not tired at all.
There is the Pollock, white, harm
will not fall, his perfect hand

and the many short voyages. They'll
never fence the silver range.
Stars are out and there is sea
enough beneath the glistening earth
to bear me toward the future
which is not so dark. I see.

(CP, p. 260)

As Anthony Libby exposits, O'Hara seems so present in his poems because "he constantly allows his visions a vital fluctuation. Always we hear his voice correcting itself, though seldom so literally as in the opening of his poem on Pollock's *Number 1*. . . . What is 'corrected' is not erased, not completely painted over, but left to enrich the general texture; the sense of acting personality comes from the poet's constant movement through various perspectives."[9] What is "corrected" is not only "not erased," in the first stanza of the poem, but serves as a model to be repeated in stanza 3. O'Hara's commentary on his own health and on the weather in the first four lines, is followed, in the first line of stanza 2 by "A fine day for seeing. I see /" and then he simply catalogues the works of art that he sees. The verb "see" has obviously more than one meaning here, since it is used twice in one short line, adumbrating what is to come. After the list of objects that he looks at in passing, he returns, in the first two lines of stanza 3, to his own physicality, substituting the word "tired" for the word "ill" used in stanza 1, but we are still located in the physical domain of "seeing" and "feeling."

In line three of the 3rd stanza, however, with "There is the Pollock," the poet turns to his perceptions of and emotional response to the Pollock painting, and to another kind of "seeing": as he is describing the painting—"white, harm / will not fall, his perfect hand/ "—he is reacting emotionally to its visual stimuli. The varying white lines of dribbled paint that flow throughout the canvas, obviously done by Pollock's "perfect hand," are juxtaposed with the numerous handprints of the painter that appear on the top, proper left section of the painting. In the first line of stanza 4, the "many short voyages," those shorter lines and small masses of darker colors that appear over the surface of the canvas and that provide its depth and "push-pull," lead to the fortunate sign of the "stars" being out, and to yet another playing with the word "see," "there is sea enough." (This also brings us back to line 7 and "the sea by Legér.") And there is enough "seeing" under the "glistening earth" to carry the poet "toward the future / which is not so dark." This is undoubtedly, in part, a rumination on Pollock's recent death and on O'Hara's sense of his own finiteness, as well as a reference to the quality of the "ground" of the painting itself. The poem then ends with the complex perception, "I see."

It is pertinent here to note that Jackson Pollock had died in a car accident in August of 1956, and that O'Hara wrote "Digressions on *Number 1, 1948*"10 on December 20, 1956, while he was a special assistant at the Museum of Modern Art, and quite probably while he was assembling the memorial exhibit, *Jackson Pollock: 1912-56*.[11] Written some months after Pollock's death, but written about contemplating a painting done by Pollock eight years before, there is an ironic quality to the affirmations "harm will not fall," and "They'll / never fence the silver range," even though the lines (qua lines of poetry) carry the aesthetic weight of commentary on the visual components of the painting. In "Digression," O'Hara re-creates the performance of the painter and of the poet, and he also provides a vital perception of some of the artistic conceptions that prevailed in the New York art world of that time. And, true to his title as the poet of "the domestic and the quotidian," he provides us, as well, through his continuously fluctuating perspective, with a weather report for December 20, 1956: "It is a perfect day, warm / for winter, cold for fall."

In "They'll / never fence the silver range" of lines 15 and 16, O'Hara refers to the impossibility of the perceptual confinement of the artist implied by the word "fence," and also, to the aesthetic concept that Pollock's "over-all" paintings were not bound by the limits of the picture plane. But the emphasis in this poem, of course, is on "seeing," and on the different perspectives and perceptions—the "presence"—of the experience.

The surety of structure in the Pollock painting, though seemingly obscured by the surface, over-all, painterly activity of line and color ("apparently chaotic and indeterminate in appearance . . ."), provides the canvas with its solid but "resonant" picture plane. And in the poem, O'Hara's structural unity carries his digressions to their final perception, "I see." "As Pollock flattened the field of his paintings only to discover the depths in their surfaces, O'Hara's flat recording of mundane existence only reveals the depths of his perception of it."[12]

Yet, as has been pointed out earlier, O'Hara's poetry is not simply a reflection of Abstract Expressionist canvasses; if we look at one of his better known poems in the light of a Pollock painting, we see both the similarities and the dissimilarities. In "A Step Away From Them," Pollock's flattened field becomes O'Hara's "flat" record of a walk in the city during his lunch hour on a particular day, and the "depths" of Pollock's surfaces become O'Hara's three-line memorial to his dead friends. Like Pollock's, O'Hara's "color" and density of line change often and range widely with his perceptions of everything that he sees, and thinks, and feels. But his space is the non-bounded area of the panorama of a bustling city, his light is the changing natural and synthetic light and shadow of the urban constructions that he passes under a hot noonday sun. And his structure is the continuity of his immediate, detached perceptions, from "It's my lunch hour . . ." to going back to work with Reverdy's "Poems" in his pocket; unlike Pollock, O'Hara's perceptions involve recognizable people, objects, places, and actions:

1 It's my lunch hour, so I go
2 for a walk among the hum-colored
3 cabs. First, down the sidewalk
4 where laborers feed their dirty
5 glistening torsos sandwiches
6 and Coca-Cola, with yellow helmets
7 on. They protect them from falling
8 bricks, I guess. Then onto the
9 avenue where skirts are flipping
10 above heels and blow up over
11 grates. The sun is hot, but the
12 cabs stir up the air. I look
13 at bargains in wristwatches. There
14 are cats playing in sawdust.
15   On
16 to Times Square, where the sign
17 blows smoke over my head, and higher
18 the waterfall pours lightly. A

19 Negro stands in a doorway with a
20 toothpick, languorously agitating.
21 A blonde chorus girl clicks: he
22 smiles and rubs his chin. Everything
23 suddenly honks: it is 12:40 of
24 a Thursday.
25   Neon in daylight is a
26 great pleasure, as Edwin Denby would
27 write, as are light bulbs in daylight.
28 I stop for a cheeseburger at JULIET'S
29 CORNER. Giulietta Masina, wife of
30 Federico Fellini, *è bell' attrice.*
31 And chocolate malted. A lady in
32 foxes on such a day puts her poodle
33 in a cab.
34   There are several Puerto
35 Ricans on the avenue today, which
36 makes it beautiful and warm. First
37 Bunny died, then John Latouche,
38 then Jackson Pollock. But is the
39 earth as full as life was full, of them?
40 And one has eaten and one walks,
41 past the magazines with nudes
42 and the posters for BULLFIGHT and
43 the Manhattan Storage Warehouse,
44 which they'll soon tear down. I
45 used to think they had the Armory
46 Show there.
47   A glass of papaya juice
48 and back to work. My heart is in my
49 pocket, it is Poems by Pierre Reverdy.

(*CP*, pp. 257-258)

32

The form of the poem suits the mood and the "voice" of the persona; the "presence" they evoke. The lineation is controlled throughout, and there are no actual stanza breaks. As the poet's walk continues, however, and there is to be a marked change of place and of pace, a line ends with a period, and the following line begins immediately following the period, but one line-space below it. Thus, there are no genuine stanza breaks that would halt the flow of continuous movement in the poem, in both the sense of walking and the flow of thought, but there are four indications of a distinct change of concentration: at the beginning of lines 15, 25, 34, and 47. So, like Pollock's Action Painting, there is control of form in the poem, as well as, simultaneously, a continuous, spontaneous, over-all surface movement.

The pace of the poem is brisk and active in the first twenty-four lines, with "hum-colored cabs," "skirts . . . flipping," "cats playing in sawdust," the signboard with an advertisement for cigarettes blowing smoke, and above it, another advertisement with a "waterfall" pouring, and then a "chorus girl" clicking. But then we are suddenly alerted to a very precise moment in time (the importance of time is adumbrated in line 1, "It's my lunch hour . . ." and in lines 12-13, "I look / at bargains in wristwatches"): "Everything / suddenly honks: it is 12:40 of / a Thursday."[13] There is a break in the pace here, as if one had come to the corner of a city block, and had to stop for traffic; the break is an intrusion, as well, on the poet's thought pattern. Beginning with line 25, the pace of the poem slows down, and the tone becomes more contemplative. We are led more slowly, and then, in line 28, the poet actually stops "for a cheeseburger at JULIET'S / CORNER." There is a momentary reflection here on the fragmentary connection between Fellini's wife, Guilietta Masina, "the beautiful actress," and JULIET'S CORNER." Then, back to the stroll, with "several Puerto / Ricans on the avenue," making either "avenue" or "today," or both, "beautiful and warm." And then suddenly, for the first time, we leave the ambience of the moving, living, active city. We enter, not another, different world of the living, but the world of the dead. "Everything" honking at "12:40 of / a Thursday" presaged as well as announced this. Rumination on the dulled illumination of "neon in daylight" and "light bulbs in daylight," in lines 25-27, led us further toward the impending shock of death in the midst of all of the urban bustle, but we are still unprepared for it. From the warmth of "Puerto / Ricans on the avenue . . ." we are plunged into the cold "earth" of death:

> . . . First
> Bunny died, then John Latouche,
> then Jackson Pollock. But is the
> earth as full as life was full, of them?

The unanswered question here is relevant to the sections that follow it. The fullness of life is re-created for us in these sections, and points clearly to the fact that the fullness of the creativeness of the artists is there before death, and that their aesthetic contribution continues after their death. We are left to wonder at the literal question itself: "But is the / earth [emphasis mine] as full as life was full, of them?"; yet, this is, obviously, a moot question. And then we return from death to life: "And one has eaten and one walks, . . ." but we return in the third person rather than in the first, which distances both the poet and the reader from death. The references to the "posters for BULLFIGHT" (a distant connection with death), and to the immanent destruction of the "Storage Warehouse," in lines 43-44, also serve as a distancing glance-over-the-shoulder at the receding world of the dead. At the end of line 44, the poet returns to the first person with "I / used to think they had the Armory / Show there. . . ." This reference to the Armory Show of 1913, the controversial art show that introduced "modern" or post-impressionist art to the United States, brings the poet back to his "world," and so back to the first person. He then refreshes himself with a drink of papaya juice, and goes back to work with a book of poems in his pocket: "My heart is in my pocket, it is Poems by Pierre Reverdy." The cliché that this phrase evokes is one used when one recalls a fearful experience—"my heart was in my mouth"—and it connotes a fear of death that the poet might have momentarily experienced as he contemplated the deaths of those whom he loved, as well as his love of life itself, and of poetry, in the paraphrase, "My heart is in my / pocket, it is Poems by Pierre Reverdy." We see here that the city and all that it encompasses, although it is the ambience of the poet, creates a situation of alienation that Reverdy's poems help to alleviate. The title of the poem, too, "A Step Away From Them," refers to the walk that the poet took through familiar city streets, and to the "Step Away" he took from those streets and scenes to the memory of his dead friends, and then to the "Step Away" from his dead friends back to his walk in the city, and back to his on-going life.

In this poem, we see that O'Hara shares with Pollock the latter's "quality of autobiographical obsession. . . ."[14] Both poet and painter are "in" their works; Pollock, physically, in his Action Painting, by actually having stood within the picture plane as he worked, and O'Hara, by re-creating the immediacy of what took place outside and inside himself without resorting to the filter and distancing of time, and without allowing an emotion-inhibiting intellectual logic to restructure his experience.

There is also a cohabitation of multiple points of view in O'Hara's poetry, as well as an intense regard for both poetry and the visual arts as "performance." In "Ode on Causality," an elegy written for Jackson Pollock, O'Hara says: make me be distant and imaginative / make my lines thin as ice, then swell like pythons . . ." and a few lines further on, "the gasp of a moving hand as maps change and faces become vacant. . . ."[15] Here he invokes the aesthetic muse of the dead Pollock ("and like that child at your grave . . .") to make his poetic lines act with the unconscious automatism of Pollock's ever-changing "lines." And he uses the horizontal correspondences of synaesthesia once again, as well as synecdoche—"the gasp of a moving hand"—to re-create the painterly and poetic processes. In O'Hara, too, there is always the natural presence of "glissando" from the language of one art form to the other, as we have already seen clearly in "Digression on *Number 1, 1948.*"

In a short poem called "To a Poet," he synthesizes some of the mutual concerns of poets and painters, and the differing points-of-view between them, as well as between poet and poet/art-critic:

> I am sober and industrious
> and would be plain and plainer
> for a little while
>   until my rococo
> self is more assured of its
> distinction.
>   So you do not like
> my new verses, written in the
> pages of Russian novels while I do
> not brood over an orderly
> childhood?
>   You are angry
> because I see the white-haired
> genius of the painter more beautiful
> than the stammering vivacity
>   of
> your temperament. And yes,
> it becomes more and more a matter
> of black and white between us
>
> and when the doctor comes to
> me he says "No things but in ideas"
> or it is overheard

in the public
square, now that I am off my couch.

(*CP*, p. 185)

"Discourse, particularly the discourse of writing, is the very essence of play. . . . The self-referential play of language is the source of ambiguity and multiple meaning. By liberating language from the definitions of reference, language at any given moment can mean or be many things at once."[16] Here, "playing" with the language of both poetry and of painting, O'Hara addresses himself to an "interlocutor" who does "not / like [his] new verses. . . ." But the author declares that he is "sober and industrious" (serious, rather than cynically humorous as he is in some other of his poems), and that he "would be plain and plainer," an oblique reference to the vocabulary of the visual arts, in a "play" on the word "plane." It is, simultaneously, also a reference to the "plain" language of William Carlos Williams. Thus the poem immediately becomes one "To a Poet," from a poet who has decided upon his aesthetic position; at least until his "rococo / self is more assured of its / distinction." "Rococo"—the very opposite of "plain" (also an allusion to his homosexuality)—describes a style that features "prettiness" and "gaiety," often carried out by the use of "C" scrolls and small counter-curves as seen in eighteenth century Louis XV furniture. And it describes a literary style that is "light, gay and graceful, and perhaps embellished by elegant twirls and flourishes of wit, image or verbal dexterity."[17] But O'Hara does not say that he wants to *change* his "rococo / self," only that he would have that self more self-assured. After this combining of a visual and a verbal style to describe his present "self," comes the question/statement to the interlocutor-poet who is obviously less than impressed with the writer's current poetry: "So you do not like / my new verses. . . ." It has been said that O'Hara was too involved with and impressed by the Abstract Expressionists and their art, and the interlocutor, "you," here may be taken to be one (perhaps John Ashbery) or a composite of those poets of his acquaintance, who felt similarly.[18] The interlocutor is "angry" because O'Hara sees "the white-haired genius of the painter" as being "more beautiful" than the "stammering vivacity" of the poet's "temperament." The "white-haired genius" is, of course, Willem de Kooning, the acknowledged leader of the Abstract Expressionist movement in New York, and another of O'Hara's "heroes," but this is also an outright statement by O'Hara of his artistic and poetic preferences, at that time. Then, "it becomes more a matter / of black and white between us," works as a cliché that implies that lines are drawn; "wrong" and "right," or at least sharply differing opinions, are defined.

But "black and white" leads us also to the notable black and white Abstract Expressionist canvasses of Franz Kline, well known to O'Hara, and perhaps even more pointedly, it leads us back to the black and white period of Jackson Pollock in the year 1951, in which he created *Echo*, *Number 27*, and *Black and White Painting*. In this poem, using the "self-referential play of language," O'Hara expresses his aesthetic point-of-view concerning the relativity of poetry and of the visual arts, and also allows his reader to become a part of the actual complex artistic milieu of New York City of that time.

Then, he abruptly shifts to poetics: "when the doctor comes to / me he says 'No things but in ideas.'" Williams' dictum, "no ideas but in things," is reversed here, but only when the "doctor" comes *to O'Hara*. Williams' "plain" language had a strong influence on O'Hara, and Williams was another of his "heroes,"[19] so the reversal here has an ironic twist, since it is qualified in the next three lines: "or it is overheard / in the public / square, now that I am off my couch." These lines are possibly among the most cynically satiric lines in O'Hara's canon, and among the most obvious of those few references to a "public," and to a "public" as "square."[20] The "public / square" as an open forum is, of course, the denotative meaning here, but the connotative meaning evokes the inference that some poets and/or poet-critics have said that O'Hara has reversed Williams' dictum in his

38

poetry—"and yes, / it becomes more a matter / of black and white between us . . ."—and thus is overly influenced by the "ideas" of his Abstract Expressionist friends. The "doctor," and "now that I am off my couch," of course, can point to Williams' influence on O'Hara (and to the doctor's or psychiatrist's "couch"), as well as to the opinion of some, that O'Hara has left the "couch" of the poets and now sits at the feet of the visual artists. His cynicism here answers that accusation by *not* answering it; he only satirically states the accusation in his own terms: "you are angry," and then points to the "*stammering* [emphasis mine] vivacity / of / your temperament. . . ." And, if we return to line 2, "and would be plain and plainer," we see that O'Hara had indeed set his own course at the beginning of the poem; the rest of the poem addresses only the objections of "others," and, in that sense, the accusations are answered *before* they are stated. Being "sober and industrious," O'Hara had decided to be as "plain" as it was possible for him to be; that is, "plain" in Williams' sense, and "plane" in the sense of the Abstract Expressionist freedom of movement over the picture plane. And he implies that he wishes to be "plain and plainer" until he is more self-assured concerning his "rococo" poetic dexterity (and his "rococo" self-hood), as well as concerning his dexterity in absorbing the aesthetics of the visual artists, and in using both to produce his own unique art form.

"Ode to Willem de Kooning," one of O'Hara's longer and more "formal" poems (*CP*, pp. 283-285), was written one year after the death of Jackson Pollock, and a year after O'Hara wrote "Digression" and "A Step Away From Them." It was written three years after he wrote "To a Poet." O'Hara is in a more somber mood here, but he continues to address the same aesthetic concerns. He is more in-and-out of this poem, however, than he is in "To a Poet," where he makes direct statements to, and asks direct questions of an interlocutor. The "vital fluctuations" of his "visions" are in evidence in this "Ode," and we have an interior monologue directed to, or at, Willem de Kooning. The poem is clearly a paean to de Kooning the artist and the man, and it clearly expresses O'Hara's hope of learning from him and of emulating him. It alludes throughout to isolated aspects of de Kooning's paintings, and in lines 5-15, speaks directly to both artist and to the man, in a language and tone of respect and deference:

> 5 and just before the last lapse of nerve which I
>   am already sorry for,
> 6 that friends describe as "just this once" in a
>   temporary hell, I hope
> 7 I try to seize upon greatness
> 8 which is available to me
> 9   through generosity and
> 10   lavishness of spirit,
>   yours
> 11 not to be inimitably weak
> 12 and picturesque, myself
> 13   but to be standing clearly
> 14   alone in the orange wind
> 15 while our days tumble and rant through Gotham and the
>   Easter narrows

In spite of the ambiguity of reference in lines 7-12, the poet clearly recognizes his debt to the "greatness" and largesse of de Kooning, and he also says that he *hopes* that he tries to use his own available "greatness" in order to be strong enough not to imitate, and so to be inimitable himself. And he hopes not to be "picturesque." (The "hope" of line 6 also refers backward to "just this once in a temporary hell" of line 5.) This last is a reference both to being unduly influenced by the aesthetic of the "picture," or by painting, and also to what he calls his "rococo / self" in "To a Poet." He wants to stand "alone" in the "orange wind," a reference to one of the three predominant colors (variations of a rose-red, yellow-ochre-orange, and cerulean blue) in de Kooning's *oeuvre*. It is also an allusion to O'Hara's poem, "Oranges: 12 Pastorals," in which the word "orange" never appears.[21]

In spite of wanting "to be standing clearly / alone," the poet continues with "while *our* [emphasis mine] days tumble and rant through Gotham and the Easter narrows," a reference to "Gotham" as an alternative term for Manhattan, and "the Narrows," the Verrazano Narrows between Brooklyn and Staten Island, as well as positing a reference to two of de Kooning's paintings, *Gotham News* (1955-56), and *Easter Monday* (1956).[22] The poet sees distinctly both his debt to de Kooning, and his own need, as a poet, to stand "alone."

Again, in lines 19-27, the poem speaks to de Kooning's leadership in the arts:

19 and I look to the flags
20 in your eyes as they go up
21   on the enormous walls
22   as the brave must always
                                        ascend
23 into the air, always the musts
24 like banderillas dangling
25 and jingling jewellike amidst the red drops on the
            shoulders of men
26 who lead us not forward or backward, but on as we must
            go on
27   out into the mesmerized world

The poet looks to the eyes, and to the "vision," of the artist for guidance in bravely overcoming the barriers that both "must always ascend" in their separate arts. The word "musts," "jingling jewellike amidst the red drops on the shoulders of men," refers again to a de Kooning color, red or "rose," and then to de Kooning's opinion that "the shoulder was a ridiculously planned part of the body."[23] "[T]he musts / like banderillas dangling" is also an allusion to the decorated darts thrust into the shoulders of the bull in the bull ring, to spur him on. Yet the "musts" of art "jingling jewellike . . . on the shoulders of men" cannot lead only "backward" to tradition, nor only "forward" toward the new, "but on as we must go on," toward the new, based, at least to some degree, upon the old.

Unlike Pollock, who "unloaded the identifiable traditional features of his art" in the interest of freedom, de Kooning drew from both traditional and contemporary concepts, and "implemented his own abstract expression with disembodied fragments of traditional art."[24] O'Hara, too, despite the "unorthodox" techniques and postmodern perspectives that define his poetry, drew from poetic tradition, and "disembodied fragments of traditional art" are clearly in evidence in this poem. In the 2nd and 3rd stanzas of the second section of this tripartite ode, lines 44-58, O'Hara uses allusions to traditional poetry, as well as to de Kooning's contemporary paintings. His language, syntax, and meter here unite the traditional and the current in the "performance" and in the "presence" of the tone of the poem:

> 44 In this dawn as in the first
> 45 it's the Homeric rose, its scent
> 46 that leads us up the rocky path
> 47 into the pass where death
> 48 can disappear or where the face
> 49 of future senses may appear
> 50 in a white night that opens
> 51 after the embattled hours of day
>
> 52 And the wind tears up the rose
> 53 fountains of prehistoric light

54 falling upon the blinded heroes
55 who did not see enough or were not
56 mad enough or felt too little
57 when the blood began to pour down
58 the rocky slopes into pink seas

In lines 44 and 45, the allusion to Homer's "rosey-fingered dawn" is clear, as well as the allusion to de Kooning's "rose." Homeric allusions and allusions to classical drama continue throughout this section, in words and phrases such as "rocky path," "the pass where death / can disappear," "embattled," "prehistoric light," "blinded heroes / who did not *see* [emphasis mine] or were not / *mad* [emphasis mine] enough," "blood began to pour," "rocky slopes," and "pink [Homer's 'wine-dark' and de Kooning's 'rose'] seas." Relying upon both traditional and contemporary figurative language, O'Hara presents us with a visual and poetic image of the battle in which the artist of every century must engage, against the opposing forces of those who cannot or will not "see."

The first two sections of the "Ode" address the weaknesses that the poet tries to and hopes that he is able to avoid, the quality of strength he finds in de Kooning himself, as well as in his art, and they address the pitfalls both poet and artist must strive to circumvent. In the third section, in lines 59-65, "Dawn" is emphasized: the rising light of aesthetic vision that will eliminate the errors of "darkness":

59 Dawn must always recur
60   to blot out stars and the terrible
                         systems
61 of belief
62   Dawn, which dries out the web so the wind can
              blow it,
63   spider and all, away

64 Dawn,
65   erasing blindness from an eye inflamed, . . .

Then, in lines 73-84, the final lines of the poem, the focus returns to de Kooning himself, and to his art:

73 A bus crashes into a milk truck
74   and the girl goes skating
                                    up the avenue
75 with streaming hair
76   roaring through fluttering newspapers
77 and their Athenian contradictions
78   for democracy is joined
79 with stunning collapsible savages, all natural and re-
          laxed and free

80 as the day zooms into space and only darkness lights our
          lives,
81 with few flags flaming, imperishable courage and the
          gentle will
82 which is the individual dawn of genius rising from its bed

83 "maybe they're wounds, but maybe they are
          rubies"
84   each painful as a sun

"[T]he girl," in line 74, is a reference to de Kooning's famous series of paintings, each painting called *Woman*, with different numerical designations. These are his grotesquely humorous, abstract expressionist figurations of a woman, always with enormous breasts, variations of a comically seductive leer on her face, and wildly colored anatomical parts.[25] The painter has said that his inspiration for the series was the billboards, and the signs on busses and mail trucks in New York, depicting huge-breasted young women with a sexually inviting smile on their face. "A bus crashes into a milk truck" and of course the picture of the "girl . . . / with streaming hair" skates "up the avenue" and roars "through fluttering newspapers"; the newspapers that undoubtedly litter New York streets. O'Hara's syntax allows for her and her "streaming hair" to also roar "through [be pictured in] fluttering newspapers."

"[N]ewspapers" leads to a terse commentary on fifth century (B.C.) Athens, the birthplace of "Democracy," and the Protagorean principle that "man is the measure of all things," as well as to the "contradictions" of that principle, in the tarnished image of "democracy" that one sees in the daily newspaper. "Democracy is *joined* [emphasis mine]/ with stunning collapsible savages, all natural and relaxed and free . . . ," a reference to both de Kooning's *Woman*, and to the often less-than "ideal" citizens of a democracy ("collapsible savages"), as well as to the more "democratic" and realistic Greek sculpture of the fourth and third centuries (B.C.), "all natural and relaxed and free. . . ." The increased space between lines 79 and 80 indicates some change in the direction of thought, but the lower case "a" in "as" at the beginning of line 80, and the comma at the end of the line, also indicate that line 79 is enjambed. Therefore the "stunning collapsible savages" are "all natural and relaxed and free" when ". . . only darkness lights our lives. . . ." (Surely an ironic reflection on Whitman's "The friendly and flowing savage, who is he? / Is he waiting for civilization, or past it and mastering it?" in "Song of Myself," paragraph 39.) But line 80 has a double purpose, since it not only looks backward to line 79, but leads the poem forward to lines 81-84.

"As the day zooms into space and only darkness lights our lives, /" the "imperishable courage and the gentle will /" become the "individual dawn of genius" of de Kooning "rising" on the horizon of art. These lines also refer to the "darkness" of "democracy," with only the light of a "few flags flaming." The "few flags flaming" refers us back to lines 19 and 20, "and I look to the flags / in your eyes . . . ," so there is also the hope that the dawn of the "courage" and the "will" of the "genius" of the "individual," in the Athenian sense, will now rise "from its bed. . . ." "[M]aybe they're wounds, but maybe they are rubies," enclosed in quotation marks, refers back to the "musts" of the artist, in the second section of the poem, "jingling jewellike amidst the red drops on the shoulders of men." (It probably also refers to "Dawn," repeated three times in lines 59-64 of the final section of the poem.) This again refers to the tones of the color red, prevalent in de Kooning's paintings, and the poet, or the artist, or both together, muse on "wounds" and "rubies," each being "painful as a sun"—painful as a sunburn on those "ridiculous" shoulders, as de Kooning referred to them? painful as the "wounds" of the "musts" (as in "banderillas," in line 24) of the artists? painful as each new "dawning"? the painfully gained successes ("rubies") of the artists? the painfulness of having a "s[o]n," or follower in the arts? or perhaps simply the pain of the (sun) light of "seeing."

In this poem, with its everpresent deliberate ambiguity, we hear O'Hara's "voice correcting itself" over and over, we see the "vital fluctuations" of his vision, and, as in de Kooning's Abstract Expressionist paintings, we sense the "constant and never-finished process of movement, development and change."

The process of development and change, with relation to the visual arts and to O'Hara's poetry is exhibited, in a different sense, in a poem in which the poet reflects upon the late "abstract" painting, *Washington Crossing the Delaware*, by his close friend Larry Rivers, done in 1953. In this canvas, Rivers' subject is the well-known historical painting, *Washington Crossing the Delaware* (1851), by the German artist Emanuel Leutze, which hangs in the Metropolitan Museum of Art. As Suzanne Ferguson points out, both Rivers' painting and O'Hara's poem "demonstrate how their artists interpret, by imitation and distortion, the techniques earlier artists devised to glorify individuals or passages from history. Both works recognize and respond to the complex but well understood systems for presenting a heroic vision of the culture in visual and literary art from classical times, systems continuously evolving through western history."[26] And, indeed, the artists' responses in both painting and poem present a vision that is a good deal less than heroic.

In the Rivers painting, Washington "lacks not only a horse, but even a hat or wig. . . , and the paint is applied with consummate disregard for the virtuosic representational styles of earlier heroic art."[27] O'Hara's poem, "On Seeing Larry Rivers' *Washington Crossing the Delaware*,"[28] presents Washington as even less a hero, and reflects on the "scene with considerably greater cynicism than Rivers."[29] In the first stanza, O'Hara says:

> Now that our hero has come back to us
> in his white pants and we know his nose
> *trembling* like a flag under fire,
> we see the calm cold river is *supporting*
> *our forces*, the *beautiful* history [emphasis mine].

And the final lines read, "Don't shoot until, the white of freedom glinting / on your gun barrel, you see the general fear."

Both the poem and the painting serve to exhibit a process of development and change in our perception of historical/mythical codes, in their depiction of the American hero, George Washington, as an ordinary figure (no horse, no hat, no wig, in the painting; a "trembling" nose, and "general fear"—allusions to a *lack* of heroism— in the poem). O'Hara's close immersion in the visual arts is once again exhibited here, in his perception of the painting with reference to the "historic" event, as well as in the poetic "performance" of his consciousness of continuously evolving societal attitudes and codes.

The language of the visual arts, as we have seen above, a language that O'Hara used in his daily work experience, often employs a specialized diction. The use of that language in his poetry, therefore, results in a poem that is somewhat "distanced," and less intimate in tone than are some others in his canon. In the two poems to be considered below, however, O'Hara uses this specialized diction to a different purpose, and it results in poems that are indeed personal in tone and mood, yet less personal than their implicit content would otherwise cause them to appear. We see in these poems the fusion of the language of art with the implicit subject matter of homosexual love, and we see the aesthetic results of that fusion.

Two of the numerous love poems that O'Hara wrote for the dancer, Vincent Warren—"To You," and the better known "Having a Coke With You"—combine the depth of erotic feeling that the poet had for the person addressed as "you" in both poems, with the impersonal diction of his art-world ambience. This results in the lovers becoming, in the poem, part of a picture—objects of art—and it also results in their near ambiguity of gender.

In "To You," dedicated to Vincent Warren,[30] O'Hara uses the metaphor of landscape painting, but that metaphor is also informed by Abstract Expressionist and surrealistic overtones:

1 What is more beautiful than night
2 and someone in your arms
3 that's what we love about art
4 it seems to prefer us and stays

5 if the moon or a gasping candle
6 sheds a little light or even dark
7 you become a landscape in a landscape
8 with rocks and craggy mountains

9 and valleys full of sweaty ferns
10 breathing and lifting into the clouds
11 which have actually come low
12 as a blanket of aspirations' blue

13 for once not a melancholy color
14 because it is looking back at us
15 there's no need for vistas we are one
16 in the complicated foreground of space

17 the architects are most courageous
18 because it stands for all to see
19 and for a long long time just as
20 the words "I'll always love you"

21 impulsively appear in the dark sky
22 and we are happy and stick by them
23 like a couple of painters in neon allowing
24 the light to glow there over the river

                              (*CP*, pp. 342-343)

The poem opens on the unabashedly romantic note of "night /
and someone in your arms," but in line 3 it suddenly distances to "art,"
and in line 4, to the reason why the lovers "love" art: "*it seems to prefer
us and stays*" [emphasis mine]. In the very first stanza of this six-
quatrain love poem, we are presented with one of the major problems
in the life of the urban homosexual: the necessary randomness and
non-permanence of the relationship between gay lovers. Here, however, that non-permanence is compared with the "permanence" of art,
which "stays," and the reader is thereby distanced from the poet's
implicit meaning.

In stanza 2, the metaphor of landscape painting is used—with the "moon" and "a gasping candle" to bring us back to the romantic mood—to describe the sexual anatomy of the lover as "a landscape in a landscape / with rocks and craggy mountains," and the description continues into the first line of the 3rd quatrain, "valleys full of sweaty ferns." The direct sexual reference of these lines is not at first perceived as being explicit, only because it is "painted" in the terms of the visual arts, and so made to seem more sensuous than sensual. O'Hara uses the language of art here as a means of expressing his deepest emotions in an alternate language that would be clear to those who were a part of his world, but in a language that would also completely carry the poem on a poetic level for those who were not. This language, therefore, was sedimented yet not oppositional. It would not, in 1959 when the poem was written, make the poet immediately anathema, nor would it make him an outright revolutionary, to a reader outside of his extended circle of non-academic poets and abstract expressionist painters.[31]

In lines 10-12, the "sweaty ferns" are "breathing and lifting to the clouds" that have "come low" "*as* [emphasis mine] a blanket of aspirations' blue. . . ." Because the actual sexual actions expressed in these lines are phrased in the alternate terms of the romantic landscape as well as in terms of Abstract Expressionist and surrealistic canvasses (e.g., "sweaty ferns / breathing and lifting into the clouds," "a landscape in a landscape"), the reader may choose to ignore them without losing the tone and mood of the poem as a traditional love poem. "Blue," usually used by O'Hara in a negative sense, is used here in the sense of the sky "as a blanket,"—*as* a blanket—which works in the terms of landscape, and also in the reversed literal sense of a blanket on a bed, as well as in the sense of one lover being "covered" by the "aspirations' blue" of the other. ("[B]lue," here, works as both the last word of line 12, and as the first word [in meaning] of line 13.) And "aspirations' blue," with "aspirations" used as a plural possessive, refers back to "clouds" billowing or blowing as in a landscape, as well as being a reference to "aspirations" in a "play" on the word "blue," the slang term for fellatio. The word "aspirations"' also refers to the strong desire of achieving a goal; that goal here, as the play-on-words indicates, is the achievement of orgasm.

In this poem, O'Hara comes close to another of his "heroes," one of the three American poets whom he mentions with praise in "Personism," Walt Whitman.[32] In "When I heard at the Close of Day," from *Calamus*, Whitman tells of his joy at the impending arrival of his friend and lover, and of his happiness when his friend "lay sleeping by" him that night:

> And when I thought how my dear friend my lover was
>   on his way coming, O then I was happy,
>   . . . .
> . . . and with the next [day] at evening came my friend,
>   . . . .
> I heard the hissing rustle of the liquid and sands as
>   directed to me whispering to congratulate me,
> For the one I love most lay sleeping by me under the
>   same cover in the cool night,
> In the stillness in the autumn moonbeams his face was
>   inclined toward me,
> And his arm lay lightly around my breast—and that
>   night I was happy.[33]

Whitman, of course, does not use the language of the visual arts here, but he is writing in the tradition of the Romantic poet. Many of his words also re-appear in O'Hara's "To You": under the "cover," "moonbeams," "night," etc. Whitman also does not include explicit details of homosexual love, but he makes the sense of a loving relationship, rather than *just* a friendship, or *just* a sexual relationship, quite clear. (While the historical ambiguity of the sexual content of many of Whitman's poems is noted, the explicit gender references of "When I

(While the historical ambiguity of the sexual content of many of
Whitman's poems is noted, the explicit gender references of "When I
Heard at the Close of Day" make the meaning of the above line
obviously homosexual in content.) And, while Whitman's concept of
"democracy" is more inclusive than is O'Hara's, both poets felt that all
things can be made "illustrious," to use Whitman's term, in poetry.

But, returning now to line 15 of "To You," we are still in the
aesthetically controlled atmosphere of the landscape painting: "there's
no need for vistas we are one. . . ." The lovers themselves *are* a vista,
and the lovers are also "one"; yet the sexual implications do not overtly
intrude on the reading of the poem as a part of the Romantic tradition
of love poetry.

Stanza 5 makes implicit ithyphallic references in lines 18 and 19,
but these references are bounded, and so restrained, by the reference
to the "architects" of that anatomy in line 17, and by "the words 'I'll
always love you,'" in line 20. The poem ends,

> and we are happy and stick by them
> like a couple of painters in neon allowing
> the light to glow there over the river

which can be read as a night scene in a romantic cityscape or in a
surreal/abstract painting, as a declaration of "everlasting" love, or as
a sedimented, extremely intimate, immediate, and personal physical
description. The pace of this poem is one of continual flow: there is no
punctuation and the only pauses are stanzaic, so that the poem
progresses toward its conclusion, as do the lovers to theirs, but the flow
is always within the framework of the aesthetic landscape.

So, while O'Hara writes an erotic poem of homosexual love, his
use of the diction and metaphor of the visual arts structures the poem
so that it "performs" as an implicitly sexual poem, or as a romantic love
poem, or as both simultaneously.

particularly in the second half of the poem, are more specifically related to particular works of art, rather than to creating a metaphorical ambience. The poem speaks in sensual tones, yet while the sexual references of "To You" are absent, still the reader "feels" the erotic emotionality of the poet concerning the male "You" who is addressed. And the direct references to works of art, in this instance, increase that feeling by expanding upon it, rather than neutralize the emotion in the erotic/homosexual content of the poem, as does the language of the visual arts in "To You."

HAVING A COKE WITH YOU

2 is even more fun than going to San Sebastian, Irun,
    Hendaye, Biarritz, Bayonne
3 or being sick to my stomach on the Travesera de Gracia
    in Barcelona
4 partly because in your orange shirt you look like a
    better happier St. Sebastian
5 partly because of my love for you, partly because of
    your love for yoghurt
6 partly because of the fluorescent orange tulips around
    the birches
7 partly because of the secrecy our smiles take on before
    people and statuary
8 it is hard to believe when I'm with you that there can
    be anything as still
9 as solemn as unpleasantly definitive as statuary when
    right in front of it
10 in the warm New York 4 o'clock light we are drifting
    back and forth
11 between each other like a tree breathing through its
    spectacles

12 and the portrait show seems to have no faces in it at
        all, just paint

13 you suddenly wonder why in the world anyone ever did
        them

14   I look

15 at you and I would rather look at you than all the
        portraits in the world

16 except possibly for the *Polish Rider* occasionally and

        anyway it's in the Frick

17 which thank heavens you haven't gone to yet so we can
        go together the first time

18 and the fact that you move so beautifully more or less
        takes care of Futurism

19 just as at home I never think of the *Nude Descending a
        Staircase* or

20 at a rehearsal a single drawing of Leonardo or
        Michelangelo that used to wow me

21 and what good does all the research of the Impression-
        ists do them

22 when they never got the right person to stand near the
        tree when the sun sank

23 or for that matter Marino Marini when he didn't pick the
        rider as carefully

24 as the horse

25   it seems they were all cheated of some
              marvellous experience

26 which is not going to go wasted on me which I why I'm
        telling you about it

                              (*CP*, p. 360)

The title, "Having a Coke With You," becomes the first line of the poem, and we are told that it "is even more fun" than traveling to distant places in the world, "partly because of my love for you . . . ," "partly because of the secrecy our smiles take on before people[34] and statuary," and "partly because" of the lover's "orange shirt" and "the fluorescent orange tulips around the birches. . . ." We are told, too, that "right in front" of statuary "in the warm New York 4 o'clock light," the lovers "are drifting back and forth / between each other like a tree breathing through its spectacles," a simultaneous use of personification and synaesthesia that heightens the sense of immediate emotion, as well as lightens it by the humorous image that is created.

The second section of the poem becomes a more direct paean to the physical beauty of Vincent Warren, the "You" addressed in the poem. The language of love is incorporated into the language of the visual arts here, and becomes a lover's continuous commentary on the enjoyment of looking at, and being with, the beloved. The homosexual references, while not overt, are implicit throughout, if only because of the sex of the subjects of the paintings and the sculpture being referred to. The subject of *Nude Descending a Staircase* is asexual, but the *Polish Rider* and Marini's sculpture have males as subjects, and the Leonardo and Michelangelo drawings can be assumed to be their studies of male subjects.

Because of O'Hara's very obvious immersion in the visual arts, the first two lines of this final stanza take on an especially significant meaning: the poet would rather look at his lover than at "all the portraits in the world." But then he provides us with a few exceptions to that generalization. And in providing specific examples of those exceptions, O'Hara actually elaborates upon his concept of the beauty of his lover. The first "possible" exception is Rembrandt's *Polish Rider*,[35] but since this painting is in a museum which the lover has not yet visited, it thus provides the possibility of the double pleasure of looking at the portrait once again, and of doing so in the company of the lover.

And the poem goes on, in lines 18 and 19, to say that because the lover moves "so beautifully," the poet never thinks of Duchamp's Futurist painting, *Nude Descending a Staircase*, when he is "at home." ("[A]t home," here, obviously means when he and his lover are "at home" together, since then he has the embodiment of ideal motion before him.) The reference to Futurism, a short-lived, early twentieth century art movement in which figures or machines were represented as being actually in motion, alludes to Vincent Warren's professional career as a dancer. He moves "so beautifully," and therefore obviates the need for O'Hara to envision Duchamp's, or any other, Futurist painting.[36] And when the poet is watching his lover at a dance rehearsal, he never needs to think of the Leonardo or Michelangelo drawings that used to "wow" him.

Then, in line 21, the poet questions the usefulness of the research of the Impressionists, mid-nineteenth century French painters who were concerned with the dynamics of natural light and shadow in relation to color. The implication here is that the "right person to stand near the tree when the sun sank" would be the poet's lover, and because the Impressionists obviously did not have that "right person," or someone equally beautiful, their efforts were less than productive. (This, of course, is hyperbole, as O'Hara the art critic and poet well knew, yet in its *deliberate* "trivializing" it again enhances the implicit point of the poem: the beauty and sexual attractiveness of the beloved.) The same fate befell the efforts of the sculptor, Marino Marini, according to the poet, because, it is implied in lines 23-24, the horse he chose as a model was more beautiful than the rider; one more humorously satiric allusion to the "deprivation" of the artists who were not provided with a model possessed of the beauty of the poet's lover.

All of this explicit and implicit praise of the lover's anatomy is brought to a directly personal conclusion, in the final two lines of the poem, where the poet states that he will not be cheated—as the above-mentioned artists "were"—of a "marvellous experience." And the lesson will not be wasted on the poet, which is why he is "telling you about it," or, writing the poem.

Sedimented in the seemingly straight-forward language of art and also in the rather "breathless" tone of this poem, is a deliberate message of homosexual love. In "Having a Coke With You," as well as in "To You," O'Hara deliberately speaks in the language of the visual arts, thus making the homosexual content considerably more difficult to identify; this language then, becomes part of the "alternative" gay language in his canon. Since the content of gay language is not "recognized" by the "dominant straight group," literary criticism often "refuses to *hear* gay language."[37] O'Hara's immersion in the New York art world made natural to him this "alternative" mode of poetic expression. That mode of expression also neutralizes the homoerotic content of his work, and so makes it "acceptable" to the straight culture, which eventually "legitimizes" it. Whether or not this "legitimizing" is salutary, remains a moot question.

CHAPTER III

EARLIER, DIVERSE SECRET SMILES: CAVAFY AND WHITMAN

Let us now diverge somewhat from visual "performances" to a brief consideration of the treatment of the subject of homosexuality by two poets who lived and wrote in eras preceding that of Frank O'Hara: Walt Whitman (1819-1892), and C. P. Cavafy (1863-1933). Whitman's poetry was an acknowledged and important influence on O'Hara, and, particularly in the *Calamus* poems, he expresses the complex emotional turbulence that surrounds even latent homoeroticism. Cavafy, a Greek poet who is chronologically contiguous to Whitman and O'Hara, but who wrote in a very different milieu from that of the other two poets, had no known influence on O'Hara.

His importance to this discussion pivots precisely on this "distance" from O'Hara in time and in locale. There is no consideration of literary "inheritance" here, but rather a correspondence between the literary exigencies of two homosexual poets. We see in Cavafy a poet whose life and environment were widely disparate from those of O'Hara (and of Whitman), yet who, as a homosexual, also reveals the need to create a unique poetic ambience. As a highly respected Greek poet, Cavafy serves us here as a point of reference from which to briefly explore the ubiquitous need of those poets who deviated from the dominant life style, to discover a unique poetic mode in which to express the emotions and experiences that are relative to that life style. His poetry, like that of Whitman and O'Hara, however, signifies an exploration of the ambiguity, the ambivalence, the peripheral nature of the "gay" world of his time and place; yet his mode of expressing his relation to that world is manifestly different from that of both Whitman and O'Hara.

It is important to our alternate reading of O'Hara's poetry, therefore, to turn to these two poets who came before him, and who, like him, wrote from an urban perspective. In doing so, we will see something of how the homosexual world had been previously addressed, and so attempt to locate O'Hara's particular stance through the sometimes over-the-shoulder viewpoint of cultural historicism.

Although he wrote in an earlier era than did O'Hara, Cavafy expresses gender sameness quite openly in his later erotic poems, whereas O'Hara, as we have seen and as we shall more fully explore in the following chapter, uses deliberate gender ambiguity in the poems that speak to the feeling of physical attraction or love between two members of the same sex. As Edmund Keeley tells us, "Cavafy's erotic poems are . . . uniquely avant-garde for work written so early in this century. In his quest to tell the truth about life as he really experienced it, he became the first poet since Whitman to make homosexual love a central subject. . . ."[1]

Cavafy, of course, was writing in the more exotic ambience of early 20th century Alexandria, Egypt, rather than in mid-19th century, or mid-20th century, New York City. But even there, Cavafy did not offer a volume of his poems for sale during his lifetime; he had his poems printed privately and distributed them himself to friends and relatives. Cavafy's "refusal to enter the market place even to buy prestige, may have prevented him from realizing all but the most private rewards for his genius. . . ." He was fully recognized by the Athenian literati only in 1935 after his first collected edition was published.[2]

Cavafy wrote also as part of the long tradition, documented from the pre-classical era, of the Greek attitude toward homosexuality. Horace, in the *Odes*, says that a poem by Alcaeus (620bc?) praising a beautiful boy called Lycus was thought to be the earlies literary expression of male homosexual love.[3] And the contemporary historian, Michael Grant, notes that the Greek attitude toward gender "promoted a society that was far more markedly homosexual than our own."[4]

Yet, for all the openness regarding gender in his poetry, the tone and attitudes expressed in many of his poems suggest that the homoerotic world Cavafy depicts is, like O'Hara's, one of secretly sought liasons and "secret smiles." In essence, as Karl Malkoff argues, one "would be hard put to deny that one of the homosexual worlds Cavafy creates, which he seems to know quite well, is furtive and guilt ridden."[5] So, it appears that even in the more permissive dominant culture of Alexandria, while his *expression* of his experiences in the gay world were to some extent aceptable, the *experiences* themselves were not so regarded. But, for both Whitman and O'Hara, one writing in an earlier, and one in a later time, *neither* the experiences *nor* the expression of them were acceptable.

Eroticism is a constant theme in Cavafy's canon; one of the earlies poems in which he dwells on the beauty of the male body, "Craftsman of Wine Bowls," was written in 1903 and printed in 1921:

On this wine bowl—pure silver,
made for the house of Herakleidis,
where good taste is the rule—
notice these graceful flowers, the streams, the thyme.
In the center I put this beautiful young man,
naked, erotic, one leg still dangling
in the water. O memory, I begged
for you to help me most in making
the young face I loved appear the way it was.
This proved very difficult because
some fifteen years have gone by since the day
he died as a soldier in the defeat at Magnesia.

(*C.P. Cavafy*, p. 114)

It is true that the poet distances himself here by using the persona of an artist who reflects upon the object of his craft, as well as by placing the poem in an imaginary situation in the fictive past. Yet, the tone of admiration for the male body and for the "young face" the speaker "loved" is obvious and pervasive.

In 1913, one of Cavafy's earliest poems that clearly link the poet with homoeroticism was published. This eleven line poem, "Very Seldom," speaks of an old man, "used up, bent," whose mind turns to the "share in youth that still belongs to him":

> . . . His verse is now quoted by young men.
> His visions come before their lively eyes.
> Their healthy sensual minds,
> their shapely taut bodies
> stir to his perception of the beautiful.
> (C.P. Cavafy, p. 43)

The eyes of the young men are "lively," their minds "healthy" and "sensual," their bodies "shapely" and "taut," and they are moved by the old man's "perception of the beautiful." Even in bent old age, he is still able to "stir" the young men, and to hold on to his tenuous "share" in that homoerotic world where he felt desire and love and fulfillment, and to which he is still emotionally drawn, but in which he knows he can no longer be an active participant.

In these two poems Cavafy's signifiers do promote a distancing through the use of the first person persona of the craftsman, in "Craftsman," and of the third person speaker in "Very Seldom," yet he obviously is not forced to use any earlier version of the oppositional language of the mid-twentieth century gay sub-stratum that is so much a part of O'Hara's poetic when he addresses homoerotic subjects.

As George Economou points out, ". . . it is through the successful integration of his perception of eros, memory, and art that Cavafy achieved the vision that he so convincingly expressed through so many personae in so many times and places."[6]

And the vision of eros in a number of his poems, for example in "The Next Table," and in "The Afternoon Sun,"—both written in 1918— an ambiguity about the sex of the referent is maintained in the original, whereas in the printed edition the sex is clearly male. (The Greek language by its very structure encourages this ambiguity, since it includes the subject in the verb ending.) In "The Next Table," the sex of the referent is made clear in the first word of the first line, and memory is relied upon to support the certainty of the speaker concerning his past "experience":

> He must be barely twenty-two years old—
> yet I'm certain just about that many years ago
> I enjoyed the very same body.
>
> It isn't erotic fever at all.
> And I've been in the casino only a few minutes,
> so I haven't had time to drink much.
> I enjoyed that very same body.
>
> And if I don't remember where, this one lapse of memory doesn't
> mean a thing.
>
> There, now that he's sitting down at the next table,
> I recognize every motion he makes—and under his clothes
> I see again the limbs that I loved, naked.
>
> (*C.P. Cavafy*, p. 91)

The speaker denies that he is under any illusions created by "erotic fever," or by the effects of alcohol, and firmly states that he sees "*again* the limbs that I loved, naked" (emphasis mine). Yet, there is clearly self-deception here on the part of the poet-speaker, or perhaps even the willing suspension of disbelief, since the given chronology belies the possibility of the given "reality." And so there is an insistance that this is "really" a memory, and he emphasizes, by the repetition of line three in line seven, and by using a stanza consisting only of one long line, that if he doesn't remember "where" he enjoyed that body, his memory lapse "doesn't mean a thing."

The repetition of line three in line seven is also provocative of a double "memory": not only the re-collection of the pleasure that the speaker found in the body of the "other," but also the re-collection of the pleasure that he found in his own youthful body at that very same time. This self-reflexive implication by the speaker can be seen again in the final line of the poem, "I see again the limbs that I loved, naked."

The reader is deliberately drawn into the *illusion* of memory that the poet creates here, but there is no created illusion regarding the sex of the subject. As Auden points out, "Cavafy was a homosexual, and his erotic poems make no attempt to conceal the fact. . . . One duty of a poem, among others, is to bear witness to the truth. . . ."[7] This dictum holds true with regard to Cavafy, even in 1918, but does it hold for Whitman's more diffident and ambiguous treatment of homosexuality? We will reflect further on this question when we consider Whitman below.

Cavafy again invokes memory in "The Afternoon Sun," where the persona re-visits a room in which he long ago shared erotic experiences with his male lover. Here, however, we sense that the persona is recalling an *actual* experience, since we are given specific and concrete details. The first five lines locate the poem in the present, and then (in lines six to the final line of the poem, given below) we share in the remembered details through which the speaker lovingly recovers the past. In line nine, the speaker even corrects himself—as we saw O'Hara do in "Digressions on *Number 1, 1948*"—in the interest of accuracy:

> . . . Here, near the door, was the couch,
> a Turkish carpet in front of it.
> Close by, the shelf with two yellow vases.
> On the right—no, opposite—a wardrobe with a mirror.
> In the middle the table where he wrote,
>
> and the three big wicker chairs.
> Beside the window the bed
> where we made love so many times.
>
> They must still be around somewhere, those old things.
>
> Beside the window the bed;
> the afternoon sun used to touch half of it.
>
> . . . One afternoon at four o'clock we separated
> for a week only . . . And then—
> that week became forever.
>
> (*C.P. Cavafy*, p. 92)

The realities of memory—"They must still be around somewhere, those old things"—are given an almost corporeal realization in this poem. And again, Cavafy uses repetition to emphasize what is important to the speaker: "the bed / where we made love so many times," and "the bed; / the afternoon sun used to touch half of it." "The Afternoon Sun" tells of a nostalgia for a deeply felt homoerotic love affair which ended when the expected separation for one week "became forever."

The final two poems by Cavafy that we shall refer to here were printed in 1922 and 1925 respectively, and they become far more explicit in their homoeroticism, as well as in their open recognition of what Malkoff calls the "furtive and guilt ridden" aspect of Cavafy's homosexual world. "In An Old Book," the speaker has found in the pages of a century-old book an unsigned watercolor of a young man. The poet tells us, in a sceptical intervention:

> . . . Its title: "Representation of Love."
>
> ". . . love of extreme sensualists"
> would have been more to the point.
>
> Because it became clear as you looked at the work
> (it was easy to see what the artist had in mind)
> that the young man depicted there
> was not destined for those
> who love in ways that are more or less healthy,
> inside the bounds of what is clearly permissible—
> with his deep chestnut eyes,
> the rare beauty of his face,
> the beauty of anomalous charm,
> with those ideal lips that bring
> sensual delight to the body loved,
> those ideal limbs shaped for beds
> that common morality calls shameless.
>
> (*C.P. Cavafy*, p. 117)

Not only is the sex of the subject clear, but also that he is destined for a mode of love that is unacceptable in the dominant culture; a mode of love that is considered to be less than "healthy," and that is called "shameless." The speaker senses and notes, however, that the young man's physical beauty and "anomalous charm," were obviously destined to bring "sensual delight" to his homoerotic lovers, and that this is outside "the bounds of what is clearly permissible. . . ."

In "The Twenty-Fifth Year of His Life," Cavafy becomes even more explicit about this "shameless" physical desire and the furtiveness that is forced upon those who seek it. Here, using the third person, the poet distances himself from the persona of the poem, whom he describes in line 13 as being "sick with longing" for someone with whom he has had a past encounter, someone who is "one of the many unknown and shady types"; someone who in contemporary gay argot would be called a "rough-trade trick":

> . . . His mind's sick with longing.
> The kisses are there on his mouth.
> His flesh, all of it, suffers from endless desire,
> the feel of that other body is on his,
> he wants to be joined with it again.
>
> Of course he tries not to give himself away.
> But sometimes he almost doesn't care.
> Besides, he knows what he's exposing himself to,
> he's come to accept it: quite possibly this life of his
> will land him in a devastating scandal.
>
> (*C.P. Cavafy*, p. 129)

There is recognition here, on the part of the speaker, of both the power of the "illicit" desire, and of the powerful potential for tragedy, yet he fully, but resignedly, accepts both. So, while in his poetry Cavafy feels free to describe his "unacceptable" longings and experiences openly, he clearly shows that in those experiences he is captive to the restrictions and sanctions imposed by the dominant society. Still, as Keeley points out, his exploration of the subject of homosexual love, "and his open treatment of the subject, sometimes so particular as to seem self-indulgent, makes Whitman's more ambiguous treatment appear a kind of indulgence."[8]

Indeed, Cavafy does treat homoeroticism openly, but underlying the surface candidness of his text, the feeling of subjugation on the part of those who deviate from the norms established by the dominant cluture forges a secret alliance with the quite obviously often over-whelming emotional turmoil that prompts the poet to create the poem. As for Whitman's "more ambiguous treatment," let us turn now to look more closely at the nature of that ambiguity, and to examine some poems from *Calamus*.

To Whitman, nothing, of any nature, is to be excluded from or despised in his poetry, and the consequent "acceptation," as he names it, is the basis of selfhood and of community; love is more important than doctrine. Whitman also has most often been discovered by later poets as a liberating influence, one who encourages them to speak in their own vernacular voice, to embrace the "un-poetic" subject. "The poet who wrote 'I sing myself, and celebrate myself' also rejoiced in 'singing the phallus' to express that element 'of myself, without where I were nothing.'"[9] And surely, it is through those concepts, as well as in the contexts of the city and of homosexuality, that Whitman is an important influence on Frank O'Hara.

On the other hand, however, Whitman's ambiguity in his treat-ment of homoeroticism in his poetry, and his efforts to avoid being thought of as "queer" or homosexual by his own contemporaries, is clearly recognized. He went so far as to invent illegitimate children for the purpose, and as Gay Wilson Allen comments, "Whitman doubtless believed that the fiction of his illigitimate children would allay any suspicions . . . concerning the normal heterosexuality of the poet of

Calamus.[10] In order to fully realize the need for these efforts, and for Whitman's seriousness regarding them, it is necessary to remind ourselves of the temper of his time, with relation to homosexuality. The climate regarding this "forbidden" topic in the United States in Whitman's era was repressive, oppressive, and opprobrious, and there were disasterous consequences for daring to reveal oneself or to speak openly about it. Homosexual writers, therefore, were "left with an enormous burden of 'self-invention,'" as well as with the burden of inventing a new diction in which to cloak their meaning.[11] So here again, Whitman has become a literary avatar for O'Hara.

Whitman's diction, as we shall point to it in his poetry, does indeed aid him in his attempts at circumlocution with regard to the sexual content of his poems. For example, he frequently uses the word "amativeness" when he refers to heterosexual love, but uses "adhesiveness" when his context is the subject of male emotion directed toward another male (or other males).[12]

One aspect of diction that Whitman did not need to invent, but upon which he frequently relies in his poetry, is that of the language of sentimentalism, so widely used and acceptable in much of Victorian writing, especially writing for and by women. This language is prevalent in the poems from *Calamus.* "Their sentimental surface overlies, and at least for a Victorian audience, disguises the author's homosexual intentions."[13] And almost a century later, Frank O'Hara, as we have seen above, uses not the language of sentimentalism, but the "diction" of art in which to embed or disguise his homoerotic meaning, and as we shall see in the following section, he also uses the language of the gay subculture of the mid 20th century to sediment emotions involved with the obviously still "unspeakable" subject.

Emotions in all of Whitman's poetry flow strongly and deeply. His catalogue of the physiological signs of pent-up sexual impulses in "Not Heaving From My Ribb'd Breast Only" actively engages all of the emotions, but, in the final line, the speaker denies his need for them, except as they "exist" and "show" themselves in his "songs":

> Not heaving from my ribb'd breast only,
> Not in sighs at night in rage dissatisfied with myself,
> Not in those long-drawn, ill-supprest sighs . . .
> Not in this beating and pounding at my temples and wrists . . .
> Not in many a hungry wish told to the skies only . . .
> Not in husky pantings through clinch'd teeth . . .
> Nor in the limbs and senses of my body that take you and dismiss
>   you continually—not there,
> Not in any or all of them O adhesiveness! O pulse of my life!
> Need I that you exist and show yourself any more than in these
>   songs. (*LofG*, p. 102)

Here Whitman negatively documents the external indications of his internal passion in the then-prevalent sentimentalism of the heaving breast, the long-drawn sigh, the beating and pounding of the temples, etc., yet his ultimate pronouncement is to deny his need of them, except in his poetry. The last word of the opening line of the poem—"only"— is, however, signally significant to an understanding of the meaning of his denial. Each line begins with "Not," except for those few close to the end of the poem, yet "only" is not repeated, except at the end of line nine. The implication of this is that the persona is denying each manifestation of emotion with the "Not" while simultaneously accepting it, as in not-only-that, *but-also*-this. So in the final line, in his seeming rejection of all of the passion that he has catalogued for the reader, Whitman actually could be certain that his rejection might be disregarded if the reader so chose, yet his ambiguity provides the poet with the opportunity to "have it both ways." This subtlety of the rejection-acceptance of physicality and then the final rejection of it in favor of a metaphysical transcendence, is necessary in order to disguise the underlying meaning of the affirmation in the penultimate line. "O adhesiveness! O pulse of my life!" is a most ingenuous poetic outburst in the light of the complexity of interpretation of the word "adhesiveness." Yet, the use of the words "any more" in the final line might be considered to be another Whitmanic deflection: Is the poet saying that he does not need "adhesiveness" outside of his poems, or is he implying a quantitative, and comparative, need for "adhesiveness" outside of his poems?

On the other hand, in the first poem of *Calamus*, "In Paths Untrodden," Whitman states clearly his intention to take a "different" road. The persona has:

> . . . Escaped from the life that exhibits itself,
> From all the standards hitherto publish'd, from the pleasures,
>   profits, conformities,
> Which too long I was offering to feed my soul,
> Clear to me now standards not yet publish'd, clear to me that
>   my soul,
> That the soul of the man I speak for rejoices in comrades . . .
> Resolved to sing no songs to-day but those of manly attachment,
> Projecting them along that substantial life,
> Bequeathing hence types of athletic love,
> Afternoon this delicious Ninth-month in my forty-first year,
> I proceed for all who are or have been young men,
> To tell the secret of my nights and days,
> To celebrate the need of comrades.
>   (*LofG*, p. 97)

Having escaped from the public life, from "publish'd" standards, the speaker's soul "rejoices in comrades," and he will sing only songs of manly attachment"; he proceeds, "for all who are or have been young men," to tell his "secrets," to "celebrate the need of comrades," and to bequeath "types of athletic love."

This direct expression of his intentions seems, at first sight, to be more forthrightly homosexual in tone than we have come to expect from Whitman. In essence, however, he relies here on the somewhat ambiguous formulations of the meaning of masculine friendship that he has elsewhere ascribed to the concept, to carry the weight of his intentions. He has praised male friendship in "Song of Myself" and therefore here, in the opening poem of *Calamus*, he can afford to take the risk of being clearly understood since he has provided himself with a literal and acceptable deflection of any accusation of having spoken the "unspeakable." Whitman provides himself with another such deflection, for instance, in "For You O Democracy" when he speaks of "manly love" in a poem in which he calls Democracy "ma femme," and in which there is no hint of any kind of "love" other than the societally acceptable love of companionship "with one's comrades": "I will make inseparable cities with their arms about each other's necks / By the manly love of comrades, . ." (*LofG*, p. 100).

And so, in "These I Singing in Spring," Whitman offers his readers an earthy and physical realization of the idea of "adhesiveness," despite the absence of the actual word "adhesiveness" from the poem, and here he relies heavily on his more-to-be-expected ambiguity. He calls himself the "poet of comrades," "Solitary, smelling the earthy smell, stopping now and then in the silence, / Alone I had thought, yet soon a troop gathers around me, . . ." And he shares with each comrade something of all he has or collects, but more importantly, he decrees the calamus-root to be the token of comrades:

> . . . Collecting, dispensing, singing, there I wander with them,
> Plucking something for tokens, tossing toward whoever is near
>   me,

Here, lilac, with a branch of pine,
Here, out of my pocket, some moss which I pull'd off a live oak in
    Florida as it hung trailing down,
Here, some pinks and laurel leaves, and a handful of sage,
And here what I now draw from the water, wading in the pond-
    side,
(O here I last saw him that tenderly loves me, and returns again
    never to separate from me,
And this, O this shall henceforth be the token of comrades, this
    calamus-root shall,
Interchange it youths with each other! let none render it
    back!) . . .

Whitman's urging of the youths surrounding him to interchange
with each other this "token of comrades," and above all his choosing
Calamus as the title of this group of poems, are indicative of the potency
that the poet ascribes to his token. The parenthetical lines in which this
statement is made commemorate the place in which he last saw "him
that tenderly loves me," and who will now return, and the calamus-root
becomes the symbol that of "adhesiveness." The calamus, or "sweet
flag," has long, sword-shaped leaves, and the root itself has for
centuries been regarded by some Native American tribes as "the root
of the Medicine Tree, the source of health and wholeness."[14]

There are obviously strong phallic implications in the shape and
potency of this "token," in the admonition to "interchange" it, and in the
warning not to refuse it. The underlying homoerotic intention here is
curiously underscored by the use of the parenthetical aside, and the
final two lines of the poem, referring back to lines five and eighteen
("Now along the pond-side, now wading in a little, fearing not the wet"
and "And here what I now draw from the water, wading in the pond-

side"), again emphasize, yet in a deliberately ambiguous manner, this underlying homoerotic meaning:

> But what I drew from the water by the pond-side, that I reserve,
> I will give of it, but only to them that love as I myself
>   am capable of loving. (LofG, pp. 101-02)

The poet is here the arbiter of love, and he will share that which he fearlessly stepped into the water to obtain, but with only those who love as he is "capable of loving." What the poet "drew from the water" where he last saw "him that tenderly loves me" is reserved; it is not for everyone, but for only those who love as the speaker loves.

We are observers of the speaker's plentitude—his "collecting" and sharing—in "These I Singing in Spring," of all the reaching out and the touching, the giving of all the poet has. But the final two lines distance us from the giving of the calamus root. This is specifically to be the "token of comrades," the phallic symbol of the love that the youths are to "interchange" and not "render back"; all of the other gifts are given without injunctions, and the giving is clearly described for us. We are not, however, made privy to the giving of the calamus. The implications here, especially in light of the direct reference to "him that tenderly loves me," are as homoerotic in intention as any that Whitman allowed to remain in his poetry. Yet the implications are always deflected either by the language of sentimentalism, or by ambiguity of concept, or, less often in *Calamus* than in other sections of *Leaves of Grass,* by ambiguity of gender. In a discussion of "These I Singing in Spring" published 1n 1932, Floyd Stovall pointed out that Whitman "considers himself especially qualified to be the poet of the love of comrades. . . . He recognizes two degrees of love. One, a kind of benevolence, which he bestows upon all without condition, he symbolizes by gifts of lilac, moss, laurel, and other herbs and flowers; the other is special, a jealous love which he reserves for those who love as he himself is capable of loving, and its symbol is the calamus root. The peculiar expression of this special love in the *Calamus* poems . . . has led some readers of Whitman to suspect him of sexual abnormality; yet it seems to me possible to explain the distinction here referred to without reference to such abnormality."[15] The real possibility of various conclusions is what Whitman deliberately provided us with, largely because of his expressed need to protect himself from the ignominy of revealing homosexual tendencies.

We have seen this felt need for protection in Frank O'Hara's "Having a Coke With You," where he speaks of the pleasure "of the secrecy our smiles take on before people and statuary. . . ." He speaks also of his particular pleasure in looking at his lover, but all of his implications are sedimented in his non-referential use of gender, and more specifically, in his use of the language of the visual arts. Whitman's deflections, or sedimentations of meaning are accomplished through the use of a different language methodology, but the effect is similar: the possibility of a multiplicity of meaning, and the consequent protection it affords.

We see this effect again in "City of Orgies":

City of orgies, walks and joys,
City whom that I have lived and sung in your midst will one day
    make you illustrious,
Not the pageants of you, not your shifting tableaus, your
    spectacles, repay me,
Not the interminable rows of your houses, nor the ships at the
    wharves,
Nor the processions in the streets, nor the bright windows with
    goods in them,

Nor to converse with learn'd persons, or bear my share in the
    soiree or feast;
Not those, but as I pass O Manhattan, your frequent and swift
    flash of eyes offering me love,
Offering response to my own—these repay me,
Lovers, continual lovers, only repay me.

                       (*LofG*, p. 107)

The title of this poem immediately places the reader in a particular and quite specific milieu—that of an urban setting, and one with a distinct suggestion of physical excess and of secret rites. The suggestion of Dionysiac indulgence in ecstatic sexual activity is obvious in the use of the word "orgies," yet the first six lines of this nine line poem are devoted, not to a description of "orgies," but to a description of aspects of the city that will *not* repay the poet for making the city illustrious because he once "lived and sung" in its midst. It is only in the final three lines that we are told just what *will* repay him, and only here are we referred back to the idea implied in the word "orgies." We are, previous to this, made aware of "pageants," "tableaus," "rows of houses," "ships," "processions," "bright windows with goods in them," conversing with "learn'd persons," and the "soiree or feast." These, in the sense that they may give us of ceaseless activity and proliferation, may be taken together as a somewhat rhetorical aspect of the word orgy, and of course, the implication of an "orgy" taken in this sense, deflects the underlying sexual passion inherent in the last three lines; the lines that lead us closest to the expected meaning of the word. The "frequent and swift flash of eyes offering me love, / Offering response to my own—these repay me, / Lovers, continual lovers, only repay me"; the words "continual lovers" return us full circle to the title and first line of the poem.

The "frequent and swift flash of eyes offering me love" remind us again of O'Hara's "Having a Coke With You," and in Cavafy's "The Window of the Tobacco Shop," a similar meaning is evoked in the following lines:

> . . . Their looks met by chance
> and timidly, haltingly expressed
> the illicit desire of their bodies.
> Then a few uneasy steps along the street
> until they smiled, and nodded slightly. . . .
>
> (*C.P. Cavafy*, p. 78)

In all three of these poems, gender is not made specific, yet each poet, as we have seen, encodes his homoerotic meaning within the lines of his poem through the use of his own poetic "language."

Cavafy, in his poetic canon, however, ". . . wishes to portray himself as deviant and abnormal. He sees himself proudly as a transgressor."[16] In the lines from "Tobacco Shop" above, gender is unspecified, as it is in a number of his poems, but when his poems are "correctly interpreted they are almost all openly or covertly scandalous, for they either deny, ridicule, or (worst of all) ignore the three bulwarks of respectable bourgeois society: christianity, patriotism and hetero-sexual love."[17]

Whitman, while he sees himself "proudly as a transgressor," wishes and strives in his poetic language to protect himself from the accusation of being "deviant and abnormal." His pride in being a "transgressor" lies in his "acceptation" as the basis for selfhood and community, in his desire to liberate, to embrace all. But as we have seen above, he "will expose his homosexuality through the agency of his poems; but since he is afraid of exposure, he will do so cautiously—by shading down and hiding his thoughts, by speaking in what he refers to, in 'When I Read the Book,' as, 'hints . . . faints clews and indirections.'"[18]

So, reflecting back on Auden's statement that one of the duties of a poem "is to bear witness to the truth," we see that the "truth" is indeed present in the *Calamus* poems that we have examined above; Whitman makes it profoundly available to us in a number of ways, and he leaves it to us to find it by following his "faint clews and indirections."

It is in these desires to liberate and to embrace all, and in his mode of encoding the poet's expression of them, that Whitman has had a profound influence on Frank O'Hara. Whitman and O'Hara use different means to both expose and hide their homoerotic meaning, yet both poets indicate the need for stealth and caution in the peripheral world of homosexuality. And the two poets discussed above, Whitman and Cavafy, give us insights into earlier "secret smiles"; smiles that seem to be the universal language of the gay world, the poetic expression of which we will further explore in Frank O'Hara's mid-20th-century poetry in the following section.

CHAPTER IV

THE EXPLORATION OF THE SECRET SMILE

O'Hara explored and examined numerous aspects of homosexual life in his poetry, and he expressed his reaction to some more openly than he did to others. The overtly sexual aspects of gay life were often sedimented, and thereby distanced, as we have seen, in poems in which he uses the language or metaphor of the visual arts. But, much of the homosexual content in his poetry is also sedimented in the "alternative" language of the gay community. The re-creation, in his poems, of the psychic emotion experienced by a homosexual living within the straight culture in an urban ambience is often expressed in a more "oppositional" language, and we shall explore below a number of poems that speak, albeit in differing tones, in that "oppositional" language.

An examination of poetry in O'Hara's canon that re-creates his experiences and reveals his perceptions as a member of the much less than out-of-the-closet gay community in New York in the 1950s and early 1960s, will prove this poetry to be a very personal poetic "performance." It is the "performance" of a poet who, because of his socially unacceptable subject matter, uses hidden discourse, who sediments meanings, who deliberately "trivializes," who now and then vents his anger and scorn openly, but who reveals the "presence" of the always "fenced" sexual experiences of the homosexual in a sophisticated urban environment. As we have seen in our examination of some of Whitman's *Calamus* poems, and as Edmund White points out in "The Political Vocabulary of Homosexuality," a "private" language was important to homosexuals at that time:

In the past homosexuality was regarded with such opprobrium and homosexuals remained so inconspicuous

that we faced some difficulty in detecting one another. . . .
It was an illegitimate existence that took refuge in language.
. . .[1]

The immediacy of the urban gay experience, the "presence" of the experience, and O'Hara's simultaneous perception of the experience, are the catalysts for poems in his canon that address his concerns as a homosexual. Since the locus for his poetry is New York City, and since O'Hara re-creates every detail in a continuously unfolding panoramic *mise en scène*, it is pertinent here to look at some of the different views that he gives us of that locus.

The city itself, in its constant movement and change, becoming and ending, alteration, confusion, and chaos—sometimes organized, often not—provides, beside the visual stimuli, a constantly moving "performance." The cacaphony of simultaneous sounds—the hum of autos, hustle of pedestrians, clangor of delivery trucks, rumble of overhead and underground trains, the jumble of human sounds—is part of the "performance" of the city itself. O'Hara re-creates much of this continuous din of motion by the "presence" that he reveals for us through his emotional and immediate response to the varying aspects of the urban milieu. We see the immediacy of his response to a particularized segment of that milieu in the poem, "Music":

1 If I rest for a moment near The Equestrian
2 pausing for a liver sausage sandwich in the Mayflower
    Shoppe,
3 that angel seems to be leading the horse into Bergdorf's
4 and I am naked as a tablecloth, my nerves humming.
5 Close to the fear of war and the stars which have dis-
    appeared.

6 I have in my hands only 35¢, it's so meaningless to eat!
7 and gusts of water spray over the basins of leaves
8 like the hammers of a glass pianoforte. If I seem to you
9 to have lavender lips under the leaves of the world,
10   I must tighten my belt.
11 It's like a locomotive on the march, the season
12   of distress and clarity
13 and my door is open to the evenings of midwinter's
14 lightly falling snow over the newspapers.
15 Clasp me in your handkerchief like a tear, trumpet
16 of early afternoon! in the foggy autumn.
17 As they're putting up the Christmas trees on Park Avenue
18 I shall see my daydreams walking by with dogs in blankets,
19 put to some use before all those coloured lights come on!
20   But no more fountains and no more rain,
21   and the stores stay open terribly late.

(*CP*, p. 210)

The poem obviously fluctuates throughout between the poet's perception of continuous motion, and the need for contemplative repose. Ironically, the first "action" word the poet gives us is "rest"—the opposite of action—and the second, "pausing"; both indicative of a constant need in the urban environment—respite—especially in the light of "nerves humming," at the end of line 4. But in spite of the resting and pausing, different kinds of "performances" are still present; visual at the beginning of the poem, but a visual performance that slips into the potential of action and the involvement of the whole sensorium. The eye "improvises" on the scene it is beholding.

Our view as the experience begins, is from inside the Mayflower Shoppe. At the time when O'Hara wrote "Music" (October, 1954), the Mayflower was located across the street from Bergdorf Goodman's, from the Plaza Hotel with its fountain, and from the Equestrian statue nearby. Therefore, from the poet's vantage point, the exterior view—distorted by panes of glass, lights, the "foggy autumn"—becomes not simply a static urban scene, but an active, visual performance. That the performance is phantasmagoric is made evident by the first word of the poem, "If," and by the phrase "that angel seems" in line 3: "that angel seems to be leading the horse into Bergdorf's. . . ." (The "Angel," of course, is not "leading the horse into Bergdorf's," but symbolically leading General William Tecumseh Sherman and his horse into a symbolic "victory," far removed in time and intent from the elegant "Bergdorf's." So we do indeed have a phantasmagorical "perform-ance.")

The poem then shifts to the poet, inside the coffee shoppe "naked as a tablecloth, my nerves humming." The poet's metaphoric "naked-ness" is ironically double. On the one hand, he seems to himself as undecorated, as plain and forthright as a cloth on an unset table. But that apparent "nakedness" is, like the tablecloth, a means of conceal-ment as well. His apparently unadorned openness is a mask for a more inward, more complex and threatening reality—his homosexuality covered by the appearance of conformity. In four lines, then, there are two simultaneous visual "performances."

More interiority in lines 5 and 6, and via the allusion to the fountain in line 7, we are again taken to the exteriority of the visual and moving "performance" of the city: in the Plaza's fountain "gusts of water spray over the basin of leaves / like the hammers of a glass pianoforte. . . ." Here the poet presents us with the "tone" of the "performance"; as fragile as "glass," and as diverse as the meaning of the oxymoron, "pianoforte"—soft and loud. The poet then speaks directly to the "imagined other," or "interlocutor," and points once more to a phantas-magoric view; this time, however, one of himself: "If I seem to you / to have lavender lips under the leaves of the world, . . ." This, of course, can refer to the distortion of natural color by neon lights, but there is again the sedimentation of gay language (as in the reference to being "naked as a tablecloth"); "lavender lips" suggesting the homosexual "lavender culture," and "under the leaves of the world," another reference to the necessity for taking "cover." There is also an allusion here to the Victorian practice of covering the genitals of nude male statuary with "leaves." Immediately following this he says: "I must tighten my belt," undoubtedly a mental reversion to a cliché because he has only 35¢ and so must limit the amount and choice of food he may eat.[2] But it is also another sedimentation of his homosexuality: "If [he seems] . . . / to have lavender lips . . ." he must "tighten his belt," or be more restrained, in order to avoid the opprobrium of an unaccepting society. "If" his gayness "seem[s]" apparent, he must also limit his "appetite" in the sexual choices he is "permitted" to have. Since his sexual orientation is outside the cultural mainstream, the persona is himself separated from "community" in his own environment.

And, within the shifting performance of urban presence in the poem, there is also a simultaneous thematizing of the dangerous alienation that always accompanies the urban experience. In line 5, the poet, the city, is "Close to the fear of war [global war? the "war" of living?] and the stars which have disappeared ["stars" of film and the arts, who have disappeared? planetary "stars" not visible in daylight?]." And again, in line 11, "It's like a locomotive on the march, . . ." *What* is like a locomotive? The noise and motion of the city? The "season of distress and clarity"? (This is reminiscent of the final two lines of Apollinaire's "Vitam Impendere Amori," a poem with which O'Hara was undoubtedly familiar: "Here is the season coming back / Of reason and of sad regret.") There is also a "glissando," a "slippage" here, to use Roland Barthes' terms, since "It's" becomes a performative when the pronoun reflects the immediacy of the act of writing, in the generalized sense of the word "motion." Then from this nostalgic tone of loss, we move further toward alienation in the rumination of "midwinter's / lightly falling snow . . ." (although O'Hara's "door is left open"), before we are brought back to the presence of the present "foggy autumn." "Clasp me in your handkerchief like a tear," is a request in the imperative to be clasped, or cherished, as well as a suggestion of the "tear[s]" of alienation; yet this is accompanied by the triumphant sound of the "trumpet / of early afternoon!" There is the romantic sense of celebration here, as well as the equally romantic mockery through ironic subversion, and both are equally appropriate to O'Hara's customary stance *vis-à-vis* the city. Thus the grandeur of trumpeting and the simple act of blowing one's nose "in the foggy autumn" are united in these two lines. O'Hara, indeed, provides us through his use of intimate detail and asyntactic language, with an immediate sense of the simultaneous intensity and detachment of the urban experience.

The poem then moves ahead in the seasons and another performative sequence of the signifiers of writing and representation, of the page as *mise en scène*, as well as the imagined "performance," has begun; this one imagined by the poet as taking place a few avenues away from his vantage point in the Mayflower Shoppe. The "Christmas trees on Park Avenue" are being put up, and he reflects on the future scene, seeing his "daydreams walking by with dogs in blankets / put to some use before all those coloured lights come on!" Does the exclamation point here suggest irritation with the unavailability of his "daydreams" (men, both gay and straight, are often seen walking dogs on Park Avenue), with "dogs in blankets" and the "blankets, / put to *some* [emphasis mine] use . . . ," or with the meretriciousness of "all those coloured lights"? Or does it imply simultaneous irritation *and* anticipation? O'Hara's deliberate ambiguity here transmits the welter of continual urban spectacle directly into the form and content of the poem by a kind of grammatical cacaphony. The final two lines of the poem—an unrhymed couplet in irregular iambic tetrameter at the end of a poem in free verse—suggest, amidst the brilliance of "coloured lights" a "resolution" in the form of a deliberately stated regret at the loss of fountains and of rain, and also suggest the poet's sense of alienation when the "stores stay open *terribly* late" (emphasis mine).

The experience of the motion and commotion of the city is presented as a continuous performance in "Music," both in the experience itself, and in the performative act of writing the poem. And the significance of the experience resides in the expression of "presence" and alienation, of intensity and detachment, of the tension and ambivalence it elicits, and of the spontaneity and simultaneity that are its constant accompaniments. O'Hara's use of a complex and broken syntax, of sedimented private meaning, and of unexpected, innovative subject matter given in intimate detail through the use of everyday speech—Williams' "vulgarity of beauty"—indicate the "unity of mad process" upon which he depends to give meaning, emotion, and coherence to the recreation of his experience of the ambience of New York City life.

There are three works in *The Collected Poems* that are each simply called "Song," and each of them combines the cacaphony and endless motion of urban existence with the voice of love or concern for a non-specific "you." As in "Music," each poem does not merely comment on or meditate on an experience in the city; rather, it becomes a translation "of the surface of the city onto that of the page, a translation into time, measure, number. . . ."[3]

For a poem to be called "Song," at all, suggests the immediacy of a "performance," or of the "self-discovering, self-watching . . . self-pleasuring . . ." performative act of the poet himself. The text of the first "Song" to be considered follows:

Is it dirty
does it look dirty
that's what you think of in the city

84

does it just seem dirty
that's what you think of in the city
you don't refuse to breathe do you

someone comes along with a very bad character
he seems attractive. is he really. yes. very
he's attractive as his character is bad. is it. yes

that's what you think of in the city
run your finger along your no-moss mind
that's not a thought that's soot

and you take a lot of dirt off someone
is the character less bad. no. it improves constantly
you don't refuse to breathe do you

(CP, p. 327)

This fifteen-line strophic poem divided into five "slant" tercets begins and ends with an unpunctuated question. And six other, similar questions are asked and answered, within the five stanzas, with the lines "that's what you think of in the city," and "you don't refuse to breathe, do you" repeated. The theme of the poem is introduced in the opening question of the first line: "Is it dirty," and the question is answered identically in the last line of the second stanza, and in the final line of the poem, by the again unpunctuated question, "you don't refuse to breathe do you." Composed of questions and self-engendered responses, the poem expresses only one "mood": the necessary acceptance of the "soot" or "dirt" of the city since it is part of the air that one must breathe, and the necessary acceptance of the "dirt" as well as of the attractiveness of another person, since the two qualities are also inseparable. ("Dirt," and "filth" are words that O'Hara uses throughout his canon in relation to sex, but not necessarily in a pejorative manner.)

This is not a celebratory "song," nor is it a song of despair; it is a poem that speaks to the dichotomy of alienation and acceptance. The "performance" of this peom is the speaker's effort to convince the "other" of the necessity for non-judgmental acceptance of the good with the bad, in the city as in life itself, if one is to survive. There is also a strong suggestion here that what is "bad" or "dirty" is actually attractive and exciting: "he's attractive as his character is bad. is it. yes." The poem is presented as a continuing performance that includes only slight, unstructured pauses, since there are neither upper case letters nor the usual spaces after the final punctuation of the periods. There is a kind of "breathless" continuity that the five-stanza structure elicits: each stanza presents and counter-presents an elaboration of the theme, "is it dirty."

Gay thematizing is obviously far more manifest here than in the poem, "Music." The "someone . . . with a very bad character" in line 6 is referred to as "he" and "attractive" in line 7 as well as in the penultimate line, and so one takes the poem to have a homosexual referent, in the light of the rest of O'Hara's canon. This is a folding in of homosexual meaning since there is some ambiguity concerning the referent, but the sedimentation of gay "cruising," or looking, lies much closer to the surface here than it did in the previously considered poem. This poem, then, is the immediate performance of the poet as he "translates" the "air" of the city into the atmosphere he creates on the page.

Atmosphere of another kind, and of a somewhat different presence is created in the next "Song" to be considered:

Did you see me walking by the Buick Repairs?
I was thinking of you
having a coke in the heat it was your face
I saw on the movie magazine, no it was Fabian's
I was thinking of you
and down at the railroad tracks where the station
has mysteriously disappeared
I was thinking of you
as the bus pulled away in the twilight
I was thinking of you
and right now
(*CP*, p. 367)

This "Song," and the one to be considered sebsequently, are believed to be part of a series of love poems written by O'Hara to, or about, Vincent Warren.[4] The poem, written in 1960, lends itself easily to its title, since it not only mentions a popular commercial singer, Fabian (the MS has "Eddie Fisher's" crossed out and "Fabian's" written in),[5] but the structure of the poem itself, although in stichic form, resembles the stanza of the popular commercial song, having the line "I was thinking of you" as a regularly recurring refrain. The ideas put forth here also resemble those of many popular songs that superimpose the image or idea of the beloved on the stuff of mundane appearance. What is notable here is that the squalor of the setting rubs off on the beloved and ironically makes him more, not less, attractive.

This is also one of O'Hara's "I-do-this-I-do-that" poems: "Walking by the Buick Repairs . . . having a Coke in the heat . . . [looking at] the movie magazine . . . [walking?] down at the railroad tracks . . . [looking on, or out] as the bus pulls away. . . ." But during, or after, each of these active "performances" the persona thinks of the "other," or "you." The performance of the poem, however, is one that begins with "walking by the Buick Repairs," takes us through the "heat" of mid-afternoon, then to "twilight," and leaves us perhaps later in the evening, with the final line, "and right now." This is a poem about constancy in gay love, even in its quintessential nomadism, mobility, and as here, its separations, since the speaker thinks of his love from morning until night, during all of the curiously mundane acts that one takes for granted as being part of city life. The poem itself, however, could also stand alone as a love poem from a female persona to a male lover, or vice versa, since the sedimentation here of homosexual ambience is deeply layered into the lines themselves, and so not obvious in the "presence" that the poem creates. This is, in essence, simply a celebratory poem of love, but with the same ironic emphasis on the "unloveliness" of reality as in the first "Song" discussed above.

The final poem called "Song" to be discussed here presents rather more complex qualities than does the preceding one, and it is also more somber in tone:

I am stuck in traffic in a taxicab
which is typical
and not just of modern life

mud clambers up the trellis of my nerves
must lovers of Eros end up with Venus
muss es sein? es muss nicht sein, I tell you

how I hate disease, it's like worrying
that comes true
and it simply must not be able to happen

in a world where you are possible
my love
nothing can go wrong for us, tell me

(CP, p. 361)

There is no doubt that this is a love poem, since it addresses "my love" and mentions "Eros" and "Venus," but it is not a poem written in celebration of love; its tone is closer to that of a lover's "complaint" or "lament." Yet, while the poem is in the strophic form, divided into four three-line stanzas, it lacks the lyric quality even of the dirge or the threnody; its tone verges on panic. But the voice of the persona does seek reassurance from the loved one, in the final line, that "nothing can go wrong for us, tell me." It also asks, must this unwanted condition occur, and it answers its own question: "es muss nicht sein, . . ." And what is the unwanted condition? We are given the answer in the obvious word, "disease." But we had been warned of what was to come in the first tercet: "I am stuck in traffic in a taxicab / which is typical / and not just of modern life. . . ." Being "stuck in traffic," is, of course, "typical" not just "of modern life." There were obviously "cabs" in previous eras—coaches, or wagons—that got "stuck" in mud ("mud clambers up the trellis of my nerves"). But why does mud "clamber" "up the trellis of [his] nerves" as he is "stuck" in traffic? The image here is the verbal displacement of the anxiety of being stuck and sinking in a situation which is typical to the extent that he has no control over it, and at the same time the image operates the spread/growth of both anxiety and the disease bringing it on: "must lovers of Eros end up with Venus." Here we have the sedimented homosexual or "alternate" language that answers the question of the something that "can go wrong for us": lovers of Eros, the male god of love, surely do not want to "end up" with Venus, the female goddess of love, but even more surely, neither do they want to "end up" with "Venus," the root of the word venereal, which takes us to line 7, "how I hate disease, . . ."[6] At the present moment in the poem, the persona's concern is with sexually transmitted disease, which has (and undoubtedly had in 1960 when the poem was written), a much higher degree of incidence in the homosexual world than in the heterosexual: "it's like worrying / that comes true. . . ." And venereal disease, like being "stuck" in traffic, may be typical, but it is also, finally, a humiliation.

In this poem, O'Hara has given us another performance of presence in the city. He has presented his spontaneous emotional reaction to two negative conditions: city traffic, and the over-riding fear of venereal disease. The poem is a lover's lament written in the cadence of the human voice. It speaks to the fear of deprivation of the lover that may occur because of being "stuck" in the "traffic" or "mud" of the prevalent disease of gay city life. (Again, "mud," "dirt," "filth," are used regarding sex by O'Hara, but again, the words are used ambiguously.)

These three poems express the "performance" of the city, as they express the "presence" that the city evokes in the poet, and therefore in the poetry. Here, O'Hara recreates the immediacy of the city experience, and the simultaneity and spontaneity of his own emotional response to it. At the same time, there is sedimented into the text of the poems the poet's private concern with an aspect of city life that is partially hidden and peripheral; that of the gay, or homosexual, community. All of the component qualities of the "presence" of the poet are experienced simultaneously by the reader as is the continuously changing "performance" of the city itself. And the reader has also experienced an intimate insight into the city as the locus of a significant part of O'Hara's poetic canon. We continue now, with an examination of poems that re-create distinct aspects of the urban homosexual experience.

Titled, "Tonight at the Versailles, or Another Card Another Cabaret," the following poem is a terse, ironic commentary on a negative aspect of the urban homosexual experience:

1 I am appearing, yes it's true
2 accompanied by my criminal record
3 my dope addiction and my sexual offenses
4 it's a great blow for freedom
5 the Commissioner said when he gave me
6 my card, you have proved that Society
7 contaminated you, not you it
8 and we're proud to have you on the boards
9 not to say the records, again
10 but try not to spread the infection
11 like Billie and Monk and the others
12 be a good whatever-you-are and keep clean
13 and I'll pick you up after the show

(*CP*, p. 375)

This poem, and the following one, "Homosexuality," with their satiric-ironic tone, illuminate different aspects of O'Hara's attitude concerning the complexities of the homosexual life style. These poems are clearly "performances" of the homosexual poet in the sophisticated, often hostile, and surely "oppositional" milieu of New York in his time.

And "Tonight at the Versailles" surely voices the not-so-covert hostility of the authority—in this instance the corrupt authority—of the dominant society. The persona of the poem is a jazz musician (the reference to "Billie and Monk and the others" in line 11 makes this clear) who, with his "criminal record / . . . dope addiction and . . . sexual offenses . . . ," tells of his experience with the "Commissioner," in obtaining his cabaret card. (The ms. is dated December 2, 1960, but no performance at the Versailles is listed in the appropriate section of either *The New Yorker* or *The New York Times* for that date, or for the previous one. We may assume then, that the performance took place some time before, or that the poem is referential to a general malaise in the legal system regarding cabaret cards in New York. In either case, the identity of the performer remains nebulous.) The first words, "I am appearing," place us within the performance of a performer recounting this experience before an empathetic audience at the "Versailles." The hypocrisy of the "Commissioner" is subtly indicated in his own words, quoted (without quotation marks) in lines 7-13. "[I]t's a great blow for freedom," line 4, separates the words of the speaker from the words of the "Commissioner," and that line can be taken to be either a comment by the speaker, or the opening words of the "Commissioner's" "speech," or authorial intervention by the poet, or all three. "Society / contaminated you, . . . / we're proud to have on the boards / not to say the records, again . . ." indicates the condescension of a controlling member of the straight society towards a non-member of that society, but a non-member who is obviously a well-known figure in the world of music, and who is a recording artist ("[N]ot to say the records . . ." indicates the speaker's criminal record, as well as his musical recordings.) That the speaker is gay is indicated in the line "be a good whatever-you-are and keep clean." The oblique reference, "whatever-you-are," is a condescendingly cynical sexual transference for the word "boy," as in "be a good boy," which the "Commissioner" might have said to a straight male, or for a boy/girl reference to a member of the gay community. The corruption of the "authority" is made ironically obvious in the final line, where the authority figure indicates his prurient interest in becoming part of the "sexual offenses" of the speaker—"and I'll pick you up after the show." The title of the poem, "Tonight at the Versailles, or *Another* Card *Another* Cabaret" (emphasis mine), is an indication that the incident re-created in the poem is not an isolated one.

Another poem with a similar satiric-ironic tone, but one that is directed inwardly to members of the homosexual community rather than outwardly to those of the dominant society, is "Homosexuality":

So we are taking off our masks, are we, and keeping
our mouths shut? as if we'd been pierced by a glance!

The song of an old cow is not more full of judgment
than the vapors which escape one's soul when one is sick;

so I pull the shadows around me like a puff
and crinkle my eyes as if at the most exquisite moment

of a very long opera, and then we are off!
without reproach and without hope that our delicate feet

will touch the earth again, let alone "very soon."
It is the law of my own voice I shall investigate.

I start like ice, my finger to my ear, my ear
to my heart, that proud cur at the garbage can

in the rain. It's wonderful to admire oneself
with complete candor, tallying up the merits of each

of the latrines. 14th Street is drunken and credulous,
53rd tries to tremble but is too at rest. The good

love a park and the inept a railway station,
and there are the divine ones who drag themselves up

and down the lengthening shadow of an Abyssinian head
in the dust, trailing their long elegant heels of hot air

crying to confuse the brave "It's a summer day,
and I want to be wanted more than anything else in the
world."

(*CP*, pp. 181-182)

This poem is dated March, 1954, and is numbered "5" in the MS,
and "Ensor Self portrait with Masks," is written below it. In a previous
MS, it is called "The Homosexuals," and is numbered "1," which is
crossed out.[7] Perhaps it can be inferred from this that O'Hara was
thinking of writing a series of poems on this subject, but in this one
work he addresses, pointedly but succinctly, a variety of perspectives
within the homosexual milieu. The tone of the poem is a combination
of sarcasm, scorn, cynicism, self-depreciation, and irony, but beneath,
or woven into the tone, is the sustained voice of pain.

Robert Martin, in *The Homosexual Tradition*, says that "Homosexuality" imitates Whitman's "Song of Myself" in an amusing way.[8]
While there is an obvious and deliberate Whitmanian influence in this
poem, and while there are numerous, loose allusions to "Song of
Myself," and even some of the tone of "Song of the Open Road," these
are often a reversal of Whitman's meaning for the sake of irony; O'Hara
is not intent upon being amusing here. Rather, he uses Whitman's
"inclusiveness," and turns it upside-down in a satiric and cynical
commentary on the limitations of choice that the "exclusive" attitude
of the straight world forces upon the homosexual living within that
world.

The first of the poem's eleven couplets asks a question in a tone
made sarcastic by the repetition and reversal of "we are"—"are we?"
and then by the exclamation of the subjunctive final clause. The "we"
refers to the members of the homosexual community in general,
including the poet, and it implies that the poet is talking to himself—
and to his "interlocutor"—here, and being critical of the necessarily

94

disparate, secretive, and often degrading ways in which gays are forced to go about finding a partner. That they are "taking off [their] masks," and "keeping [their] mouths shut? as if [they'd] been pierced by a glance!" is a negative questioning of their own integrity, engendered, perhaps, by a look or a word of hostility from a female "outsider" ("The song of an old cow . . ." in line 3). As Edmund White tells us, "before 1969 only a small though courageous and articulate number of gays had much pride in their homosexuality or a conviction that their predilections were legitimate. The rest of us defined our homosexuality in negative terms. . . ."[9]

Negativity is reinforced here by the notation on the MS concerning Ensor. The comment is revealing in a number of ways: first, it affirms the poem's depiction, as a "*Self portrait*," either of the poet himself, or of the homosexual community, or of both. Secondly, the reference to the Belgian painter, James Ensor, who worked at the end of the nineteenth century and during the first half of the twentieth, tells us what kind of a self portrait it is. Ensor's paintings have a strangely macabre quality, and he often uses masks and skeletons to depict his pessimistic view of human-kind. *Intrigue,* for example, painted in 1890, is a "grotesque carnival" in which all of the participants wear masks, "but as we scrutinize these masks we become aware that they are the mummers' true faces, revealing the depravity ordinarily hidden behind the facade of everyday appearances."[10] So the self portrait of "Homosexuality," as presaged in the first two lines of the poem, will be a negatively self-critical one.

The second couplet begins with "The song of an old cow," and while this is perhaps faintly reminiscent of Whitman's title, "Song of Myself," since O'Hara uses frequent allusions to that poem in "Homosexuality," his allusions nevertheless depend for their meaning upon an implicit understanding of and agreement with Whitman's theme. Since Whitman was one of O'Hara's "heroes," and because of Whitman's generally accepted historical reputation as at least a latent homosexual, we may assume that O'Hara does understand and does agree with Whitman's theme that *all* things may be "illustrious," and, relying upon that understanding, he departs, in the 3rd couplet, on a poetic journey of his own. O'Hara's journey takes him on a different path from that of Whitman's "Song of Myself," yet there is some imitation of its form and diction here, as well as a strong similarity of sentiment. But O'Hara's sentiments are expressed with such an ironic and satiric "turn," that the effect is a sardonic and negative one, rather than one of all-encompassing acceptance.

So, in the lines, "The song of an old cow is not more full of judgment / than the vapors which escape one's soul when one is sick;" we see Whitmanian diction in "vapors," and in "escape one's soul." But O'Hara turns the tone *away* from the diction here by his manipulation of syntax, and the "judgment" exhibited in "The song of an old cow" becomes only as meaningful as an escaping gas, or just "hot air."

Yet there is more than simply the use of Whitmanian diction in this couplet; we hear, very clearly, Whitman's strong belief in the equality of all men, and his opposition to those who would criticize the non-conformist. He tells us, in paragraph 20:

> Whimpering and truckling fold with powders for invalids,
>   conformity goes to the fourth-remov'd,
> I wear my hat as I please indoors or out.
>   . . . .
> In all people I see myself, none more and not one a barley-corn
>   less,
> And the good or bad I say of myself I say of them.

So in the second couplet, while O'Hara echoes Whitman's feelings, he states them with a direct and cutting irony that we do not find in

Whitman's poetry. We do see here, of course, Whitman's strong and acknowledged influence on O'Hara, as well as O'Hara's 20th-century sense of his own poetic "performance."

The poet then pulls "shadows"—dark, ephemeral, changing, like "vapors," having no quality of solidity—around him like a "puff"—again light and airy (as well as being an alternate term for homosexual) and "crinkle[s] [his] eyes as if at the most exquisite moment // of a very long opera. . . ." In paragraph 26 of "Song of Myself," Whitman tells us: "I hear the chorus, it is a grand opera, / Ah this indeed is music—this suits me," but O'Hara says only "*as if* [emphasis mine] at the most exquisite moment // of a very long opera. . . ." And in paragraph 15, Whitman speaks of "The connoisseur [who] peers along the exhibition-gallery with half-shut eyes / bent sideways," and later of "The prostitute [who] draggles her shawl, . . ." In the final line of this paragraph Whitman says: "And of these one and all I weave the song of myself." Once more the connection between the two poems is obvious, but again O'Hara uses the descriptive qualities of his poem in deprecation, not in acceptance as does Whitman, yet he does it "without reproach."

And the diction that O'Hara uses in "Homosexuality"—"pull the shadows," "puff," "crinkle my eyes," "the most exquisite moment"—has an obvious connection with the so-called light or "camp" diction[11] of the contemporary gay milieu. So we are led, step-by-step, in accompanying the poet on his critical and uneasy journey of exploration into his own world. And we find that he often looks back to the earlier American poet who took a more "inclusive," journey before him: In paragraph 46 of "Song of Myself," Whitman says, "I tramp a perpetual journey, (come listen all!)."

And O'Hara and his "interlocutor," after preparing for this "journey" "without reproach and without hope that our delicate feet // will touch the earth again, let alone "very soon," are "off!" To where? We begin to find the answer to this question in couplet 7, but the three preceding couplets set the mood for the "journey," "We," the poet and his "interlocutor," go off without "reproach"—self-reproach—but also without "hope," of his feet touching the earth again, "let alone 'very soon'. . . ." Whitman, in paragraph 44, says:

> My feet strike an apex of the apices of the stairs
> On every step bunches of ages, and larger bunches
>   between the steps,
> All below duly travel'd, and still I mount and mount. . . .

While there are "bunches of ages" on Whitman's steps, and "larger bunches" between them, and while he has reached one apex of the stairs, "still [he] mount[s] and mount[s]." Whitman is speaking of the cosmic journey of man's evolution here, and O'Hara, too, knows that the journey will be along one, since he tells us that he does not expect his "delicate feet" to touch the earth again, "let alone 'very soon'. . . ." Whitman's are not "delicate" feet as are O'Hara's, but he, too, goes "off" on his journey; and he expects not only to "touch the earth again," but also to become part of it. He says, at the end of "Song of Myself," "I depart as air, . . . I bequeath myself to the dirt to grow from the grass I love, / If you want me again look for me under your boot-soles." O'Hara, too, departs as air, since his feet are not touching the earth, but unlike Whitman, he expresses no hope of becoming part of the earth.

Then O'Hara says, in the second line of couplet 5, that on this quest, "It is the law of my own voice I shall investigate." This is the only end-stopped, self-contained line in "Homosexuality," and therefore it tells us directly that he is not investigating a "song" of himself, but the "law of [his] own voice." Is this the "voice" of his "heart"? his poetry? Or is it the "voice" of communication in the gay world? Whitman, in paragraph 24, speaks of the many voices that speak through him, and says:

I speak the pass-word primeval, I give the sign of
    democracy, . . .
      . . . .
Through me forbidden voices,
Voices of sexes and lusts, voices veiled and I remove the
    veil,
Voices indecent by me clarified and transfigur'd.

O'Hara, in this poem, is, like Whitman above, removing the "veil," or "mask," to use his own word, from the veiled "voices of sexes and lusts," and will investigate the "law of his own voice." And in that investigation he, too, will perhaps clarify, if not transfigure, "voices indecent" of his own world.

    The poet starts "off" on his journey of investigation, "like ice, [his] finger to [his] ear, [his] ear / to [his] heart, that proud cur at the garbage can // in the rain. . . ." He is emotionally "cold" as he sets out, yet his finger is to his "ear," which is "listening" to his "heart," or to his emotions, and then out of his "coldness" there comes the self-denigrating, *emotional* comparison of his "heart" with "that proud cur at the garbage can // in the rain. . . ." One senses the poet's swift change from "coldness" to the reluctant admission of the indignity, and also to the underlying anger of "at the garbage can // in the rain. . . ." This is the presaging of the exploration of gay "cruising" that is about to begin. And here again, there is the connection with, yet distancing from, Whitman's "Song of Myself," where, in paragraph 24, he says:

I do not press my fingers across my mouth,
I keep as delicate around the bowels as around the
      head and heart,
Copulation is no more rank to me than death is.

The sexual experience, as Whitman writes about it in the 19th century, is "delicate" and not "rank," but it often becomes, to the homosexual in New York City in the 20th century, a degrading experience because of the necessity to seek impersonal, secret liasons in public places. (Homosexuality was certainly not less frowned-upon by society in Whitman's time than it is today; in actuality, O'Hara can write about it with more freedom than could Whitman. But Whitman was writing from a different societal environment than is O'Hara, and also, "Song of Myself" [unlike *Calamus*], does not emphasize homosexuality. But we see O'Hara's sense of the satiric and ironic in their relative situations in his imitation of Whitman in "Homosexuality.")

And now, in couplet 7, another allusion to Whitman: "It's wonderful to admire oneself / with complete candor. . . ." This, of course, is literally referential to all of "Song of Myself," but particularly to these lines in paragraph 3:

Showing the best and dividing it from the worst age
    vexes age,
Knowing the perfect fitness and equanimity of
    things, while they discuss I am silent, and go bathe
    and admire myself. (emphasis mine)

We can see, however, that O'Hara's line is meant to convey sarcasm and self-mockery because of what follows. This is the announcement of the purpose of the entire journey: to tally "up the merits of each // of the latrines." Here, it is the "heart, that proud cur . . ." that speaks. The word "proud" has its desired effect when it becomes clear that with this pride, like that of the "cur," he will measure the "merits" of "latrines," or places for the collection of refuse. (Public rest rooms are sometimes referred to as "tea rooms" in the gay community, a sardonic twist of meaning concerning the tea room of the "straight" world as a "polite" social meeting place.)[12] The latrines of "14th Street," and "53rd" Street are the New York City subway mens' rooms: "14th Street" is downtown, in a busy, commercial, shoddy area, and so its frequenters are "drunken and credulous"; "53rd" is uptown, off the then-elegant Fifth Avenue and across from the Museum of Modern Art. It tries to "tremble," as subway rest rooms often seem to do because of the rumble of trains beneath them, and gays try to make contact, or sexually "tremble," there, but "53rd" is too "at rest"—in too staid an area for homosexual contact.

Still "tallying," the poet informs us that the "good," or those usually successful at finding (and being) lovers, "love a park," and the "inept," or the unsuccessful, choose a "railway station." And "the divine ones," the transvestites in "drag," "drag themselves . . . trailing their long elegant heels of hot air." The reference to "heels of hot air" is, of course, to the high-heeled shoes worn by the transvestites. But this is also a "sedimented" reference to the "lengthening shadow" of the black penis that the transvestites are fellating when they "drag themselves up // and down the *lengthening* [emphasis mine] shadow of an Abyssinian head" as they kneel "in the dust" with their "heels" behind them, or "trailing."

And in the final couplet, they, "the divine ones," are "crying to confuse the brave 'It's a summer day, / and I want to be wanted more than anything else in the world.'"

We come again here to Whitman, who in the final line of paragraph 25 says, "With the hush of my lips I wholly confound the skeptic." O'Hara now reverses Whitman's statement and instead of silence to "confound the skeptic," he has the transvestites "crying to confuse the brave. . . ." Whitman develops his silence and his own listening throughout paragraph 26, and O'Hara alludes to the lines below in his final couplet:

I hear the sound I love, the sound of the human voice,
I hear all sounds running together, combined, fused or
      following,
Sounds of the city and sounds out of the city, sounds of
      the day and night, . . .

      . . . .

The angry base of disjointed friendship, . . .

      . . . .

I am cut by bitter and angry hail, I lose my breath, . . .
At length let up again to feel the puzzle of puzzles,
And that we call Being.

In this paragraph Whitman listens to all of the sounds of life and is brought, by the totality of the experience, to something beyond the senses. O'Hara, however, ironically reverses Whitman in the final couplet of "Homosexuality," and has the transvestites *making the sounds* "to confuse the brave," and Whitman's "puzzle of puzzles," "Being," becomes O'Hara's confusion of "being" in the homosexual world, in the cry of the transvestites: "It's a summer day, / and I want to be wanted more than anything else in the world." O'Hara borrows loosely from Whitman here, as he does throughout this poem, and he condenses Whitman's cataloguing to his own purposes. The "sound of the human voice / . . . all sounds running together . . . Sounds of the city . . . The angry base of disjointed friendship . . ." all these are implicit, but reversed, in the cry of the "divine ones" since they are "crying to confuse the brave"; they are not being silent to "confound the skeptic."

They cry "to *confuse* the brave" (emphasis mine). The poem began with "So we are taking off our masks, are we . . ." and the different types of homosexual "masks" have been taken off by the poet on this journey. Now, in couplet 11, those who wear the most obvious "masks," the transvestites, try to "confuse the brave"—those who do not wear them.

They cry, "I want to be wanted more than anything else in the world," which to the "brave"—those who take the risk of a permanent *loving* relationship in the random world of homosexuality—would mean that they actually want to be "loved." But the wearers of the masks, because they wear such an *obvious* mask, ask only to be chosen, not loved—they want to engage in random sex. Perhaps they want also to be loved, but in their deliberate and exaggerated imitation of the popularly accepted "desire" of the female sex, their cry of being "wanted more than anything else in the world" serves only to confuse. O'Hara seems to be pointed out, however, that *all* homosexuals in our society are forced to be, like the "proud cur at the garbage can," basically simply survivors.

The final line of couplet 11, and the final line of the poem, is the epitome of the voice of pain that weaves in and out of the irony of this poem; the inherent sense of the basic human need to be loved, not just to be chosen for the moment. (Lines 3 and 4 of "To You" say this in their reference to the reason for the lovers' love of art: "it seems to prefer us and stays"; it has a permanence that homosexual relationships often lack.) The final line of "Homosexuality" contrasts the not-"brave" with the "brave" who *do* "want to be *wanted*" (emphasis mine)." Yet, it also simultaneously unites them in their common need to be wanted "more than anything else in the world"; the "brave" in a permanent love relationship, the not-"brave" for at least the moment. (But there is, perhaps, also the intimation here that the cry of the "divine ones" is simply "[t]he song of an old cow," of couplet 2, that lacks "judgment.")

In "Homosexuality," O'Hara has alluded to sections of "Song of Myself" as an antinomical contrast between Whitman's ideal inclusiveness, and the much less than ideal "exclusiveness" forced upon the homosexual. Through these allusions he has sharpened the irony of his own poetic commentary on the "masks," as well as on some of the painful exigencies of living within the gay community of New York City in the mid-twentieth century. There is sedimentation of meaning in this poem, there is some use of "oppositional" language as well, but the title of the poem is explicit, the urban locus is specific, and the use of gay terms is evident.[13] Thus O'Hara re-creates, in a twenty-two line poem, the "presence" of the subterranean side of the reality of homosexual life in the contemporary urban milieu.[14]

Another, but much more pleasant side of that reality is re-created in "At the Old Place," a poem with a very distinctly "camp" tone and mood. It was written in 1955, but not published until 1969, three years after O'Hara's death.[15]

Joe is restless and so am I, so restless.
Button's buddy lips frame "L G T TH O P?"
across the bar. "Yes!" I cry, for dancing's
my soul delight. (Feet! feet!) "Come on!"

Through the streets we skip like swallows.
Howard malingers. (Come on, Howard.) Ashes
malingers. (Come on, J.A.) Dick malingers.
(Come on, Dick.) Alvin darts ahead. (Wait up,
Alvin.) Jack, Earl and Someone don't come.

Down the dark stairs drifts the steaming cha-
cha-cha. Through the urine and smoke we charge
to the floor. Wrapped in Ashes' arms I glide.
(It's Heaven!) Button lindys with me. (It's
heaven!) Joe's two-steps, too, are incredible,
and then a fast rhumba with Alvin, like skipping
on toothpicks. And the interminable intermissions,

we have them. Jack, Earl and Someone drift
guiltily in. "I knew they were gay

the minute I laid eyes on them!" screams John.
How ashamed they are of us! we hope.

(*CP*, pp. 223-224)

Though here we have a portrayal of the lighter side of the gay life-style, the deliberately "trivializing," "camp" tone of the poem is somewhat deceiving. It is deceiving because underneath the almost childlike repetitiousness and sing-song surface of the poem, this is a "seriously" happy poem. Susan Sontag has called "camp" a "sensibility"—a "love of artiface and exaggeration." She says that it also tends toward the "androgynous," it is the triumph of the "epicene" style, it is always naive and rests on "innocence," and that it is not necessarily homosexual, but "homosexuals constitute the vanguard."[16]

The homosexual aspect of "camp," however, also involves a sedimentation of "oppositional" meaning; that is, its language "covers," or hides a private meaning, one not available to those outside of the gay community. The mood of this poem seems at first glance to be one of naively self-indulgent pleasure, but it is actually one of true joy and liberation. The personae are able to remove their "masks" of conformism at "The Old Place," a gay dance-bar, and are free to be themselves. And O'Hara re-creates the "presence" of their sense of exhilaration at this freedom.[17]

The poem begins *in medias res*, so to speak, and "Joe" and the poet are "restless," "so restless." "Button's buddy lips"—"buddy" as in friend, and bud-y as in bud-shaped—"frame 'L[et's] G[o] T[o] Th[e] O[ld] P[lace]?' / across the bar." The "bar" is of course their present location; it is also the "bar" of the members of the "straight" community who are present, and so prevent open, intimate communication. The "so restless" of line 1, and the "Yes! I cry . . ." of line 3 introduce the tone of playful enthusiasm that continues throughout the poem. Lines 3 and 4 carry this forward with "for dancing's / my soul delight. (Feet!

feet!) 'Come on!'" Dancing delights the poet's "soul," but the play on words: "soul—sole (only), and the "sole" of "(Feet! feet!)"—continue the "trivializing" mood, and stanza one ends with the excited "'Come on!'"

After line 5, the syntax of the rest of stanza two is marked by asyndeton, and the form is that of the short, repetitious, declarative sentences of a child's reading primer. The traditional trochaic tetrameter, unusual for O'Hara, of line 5 (and repeated in each complete sentence of lines 11, 12, and 20) adds a tone of mock seriousness to the simile "we skip like swallows," and then, in lines 5 through 8 we have the "innocence" of the reading primer. But the stanza ends on a more seriously declarative note: "Jack, Earl and Someone don't come." This part of line 9 presages a slight change in mood, but not in tone. It is the diction in the first two lines of stanza three that creates a somewhat different mood: "Down the dark stairs," "steaming," "urine and smoke." We therefore know that, here, we are not in a place similar to the quiet, more subdued bar that we have just left. This is one that is more hidden—the music drifts "Down the dark stairs"—this is a place more "masked" from public scrutiny.

But one, we are told in a trochaic tetrameter, that again alters the pace of the poem. Once upstairs, "Through the urine and smoke we charge / . . ." and, "Wrapped in Ashes' arms I glide." Though the meter of these two statements is the same, the effect of each is altered by diction; the final verbs, "charge," and "glide," indicate the very different physical movements involved in each action, by both their meaning and their sound (the short "a" and hard "ch" and "r" sounds of "charge," and the long "i" of "glide"). And then in lines 13 and 14, we again have the innocent enthusiasm of the exclamatory remarks of stanza one, and of the child-like declarative sentences of stanza two. ("It's heaven!" exclaimed twice, contrasts with "dark," "steaming," "urine and smoke" in lines 10 and 11). Here, however, they express not the anticipation of pleasure, but the experience of the pleasure itself. From "Joe's two-steps, too, are incredible," we go to "a fast rhumba with Alvin, like

106

skipping / [this word now used in a somewhat fractured simile (cf. line 5) as a naive expression of delight] on toothpicks." Then, the mood again drops, and the stanza breaks, with "the interminible intermissions, // we have them."

After the stanza break there is another "dramatic" occurence. "Jack, Earl and Someone drift / guiltily in." The three who stayed behind at the first bar arrive "At The Old Place," looking guilty; guilty perhaps because they are still uncomfortable at frequenting gay bars, and because they recognize their acquaintances from their previous meeting, or perhaps they are "guilty" for not coming with the others. And then the most pointed exclamation of the poem: "'I knew they were gay / the minute I laid eyes on them!' screams John." Here there is the unrestrained expression of the freedom to drop the "mask"—their own and that of others. And again in trochaic tetrameter, "How ashamed they are of us!" the poet says. And he says they "hope" that is true. But also, perhaps, they hope that "Jack, Earl and Someone" are also ashamed of themselves for feeling "guilty" about the open expression of their gayness. The words "we hope" may also simultaneously stand as a thematic statement for the entire poem.

The "presence" of O'Hara's re-creation of the experience of escaping from the restriction of the straight world into a world where gays are free to be themselves, is one of simple, yet still sophisticated, joyfulness. Here he shows one way in which the members of a "subculture," internally varied as it may be, function *within* that alternate culture.

Another side of the reality of gay life, presented within the metaphors of astronomy and myth, is "Poem" [Twin spheres full of fur and noise]. It was written in 1961, at the end of what has been called O'Hara's "golden period,"[18] and the absolute lack of punctuation and connectives here is representative of his later style. This is also one of the series of love poems to Vincent Warren, and it is reminiscent of the earlier "To You" in its praise of the lover and of the act of love. And while this praise is presented metaphorically, it is not phrased in the language of the visual arts, and therefore the homosexual content is more readily available. But that content is sedimented here in the metaphor of astronomy, in allusion to ancient myths, and in an occasional play on words—as in "Odyssies" ("Oddy" sees), and in "jetting." This poem is a re-creation of one of the intimate physical aspects of the reality of gay life, as is "To You," and it was written during the time that O'Hara's love affair with Vincent Warren was ending, which is adumbrated in the final lines of the poem:

> Twin spheres full of fur and noise
> rolling softly up my belly beddening on my chest
> and then my mouth is full of suns
> that softness seems so anterior to that hardness
> that mouth that is used to talking too much
> speaks at last of the tenderness of Ancient China
> and the love of form the Odyssies
> each tendril is covered with seed pearls
> your hair is like a tree in an ice storm
> jetting I commit the immortal spark jetting
> you give that form to my life the Ancients loved
> those suns are smiling as they move across the sky
> and as your chariot I soon become a myth
> which heaven is it that we inhabit for so long a time
> it must be discovered soon and disappear
>
> (CP, pp. 405-406)

Whereas "To You" begins in a romantic tone and uses the metaphor of landscape painting to re-create an emotional sexual experience, here O'Hara uses the metaphor of astronomy and myth and the tone is less romantic and less emotional. This "Poem" also becomes less a poem of love, and more the re-creation of the eroticism of the sexual experience. The anatomical references are more specific here: "[T]win spheres . . . rolling softly up my belly . . . my mouth is full . . . softness . . . so anterior to that hardness / . . . jetting . . . as your chariot. . . ." In "To You," the references to anatomy are couched in gentler terms; there are "valleys full of sweaty ferns" and "the architects are most courageous / because it stands for all to see / and for a long long time. . . ." In this "Poem," the gentleness of the romantic landscape is gone, and there is more specificity concerning genitalia, and in the use of slang as in "jetting" and "chariot." The use of the word "jetting" as a sexual reference, of course, did not originate with O'Hara. Whitman says, in paragraph 40 of "Song of Myself": "On women fit for conception I start bigger and nimbler babes, / (This day I am jetting the stuff of far more arrogant republics.)" His sexual rererence, however, is made a clearly heterosexual one by the use of the word "women," whereas in the poem under discussion, "jetting" is used in a homoerotic context.

We also see the reference here to the ending of the love affair in "and as your chariot I soon become a myth / which heaven is it that we inhabit for so long a time / it must be discovered soon and disappear." While the language in both of these poems sediments, to different degrees, the homsexual content, it is the language of art in "To You," that sediments the sexual reality of gay life more deeply.

The final poem to be discussed in this chapter is one that synthesizes O'Hara's "performance" as a poet whose view is one that is oblique from the periphery. In the narrative poem, "Mary Desti's Ass,"[19] we have a disguised form of story-telling. Through the use of humor, meiosis, and deliberate "trivialization," O'Hara sediments the homosexual content of this poem. He relates, rather than describes, in a humorous manner, the separate but continuous experiences of the

homosexual living within the straight culture, by using generally fictive
references to different parts of the world:

> In Bayreuth once
> we were very good friends of the Wagners
> and I stepped in once
> for Isadora so perfectly
> she would never allow me to dance again
> that's the way it was in Bayreuth
>
> the way it was in Hackensack
> was different
> there one never did anything
> and everyone hated you anyway
> it was fun, it was clear
> you knew where you stood
>
> in Boston you were never really standing
> I was usually lying
> it was amusing to be lying all
> the time for everybody
> it was like exercise
>
> it means something to exercise
> in Norfolk Virginia
> it means you've been to bed with a Nigra
> well it is exercise
> the only difference is it's better than Boston
>
> I was walking along the street
> of Cincinnati

and I met Kenneth Koch's mother
fresh from the Istanbul Hilton
she liked me and I liked her
we both liked Istanbul

then in Waukegan I met a furniture manufacturer
and it wiped out all dreams of pleasantness from my mind
it was like being pushed down hard
on a chair
it was like something horrible you hadn't expected
which is the most horrible thing

and in Singapore I got a dreadful
disease it was amusing to have bumps
except they went into my veins
and rose to the surface like Vesuvius
getting cured was like learning to smoke

yet I always loved Baltimore
the porches which hurt your ass
no, they were the steps
well you have a wet ass anyway
if they'd only stop scrubbing

and Frisco where I saw
Toumanova "the baby ballerina" except
she looked like a cow
I didn't know the history of the ballet yet
not that that taught me much

now if you feel like you want to deal with
Tokyo

you've really got something to handle
it's like Times Square at midnight
you don't know where you're going
but you know

and then in Harbin I knew
how to behave it was glorious that
was love sneaking up on me through the snow
and I felt it was because of all
the postcards and the smiles and kisses and the grunts
that was love but I kept on traveling

(*CP*, pp. 401-402)

Edmund White tells us that the technique of using "endless disolves of time and geography, as though the same party were being reassembled over decades and on different continents, . . ." is a homosexual technique. "Anyone who has experienced the enduring and international links of gay life will recognize how the technique is a formal equivalent to the experience."[20]

O'Hara begins his "narrative" in Bayreuth, the city in which Richard Wagner founded his own theatre, where the first complete performance of *The Ring* was given, and where Wagner died and was buried in 1883. Wagner's son, Siegfried, was art director of the Bayreuth Festival Plays from 1909 to 1930.[21] But the "chatty" tone of this first stanza presents O'Hara and "the Wagners" as contemporaries and "good friends," and so sets the fictitious voice and the direction of the literal content of the poem. We then go immediately to the narrator's stepping in "for Isadora,"—again, obviously fictitious, since Isadora Duncan died in 1927, one year after O'Hara was born—which brings to the foreground the poet's connection with dance,[22] as well as the line's androgynous implications, since in an O'Hara poem the "I" almost always represents the poet. Here, however, the sex of the narrator/persona/ poet is not clearly identified, and this is a major element in the poem's sedimented meaning. He "stepped in once / . . . so perfectly"—*his* dancing was such a "threat" to Isadora Duncan— that she never allowed him "to dance again." O'Hara's meaning concerning the ability of a gay man to "step in" for a female dancer is clear here, but only if the reader is aware that the language of this poem is largely "oppositional"; its diction is chosen for the purpose of disguising its expository meaning from members of the straight culture.

We then go from the exotic world of Bayreuth to the quotidian— Hackensack, N.J. And, the poet says, there it "was different." Even though "one never did anything / . . . everyone hated you anyway." Even though, as one who naturally deviated from the norm of heterosexual society, he "never did anything" that would leave himself open to criticism, he was hated in that drab, ordinary city simply because he was so identified. But, because the "lines were drawn," so to speak, "it was fun," if only because "you knew where you stood."

When we arrive in Boston, however, knowing where you "stood" becomes a reference to social standing": "you were never really standing." And then, a play on the word "lying": telling a lie, and the physical "lying," as in sexual activity. Here, one lies "all / the time," about one's sexual preference, and possibly about one's social stand- ing, but also, "it was amusing to be lying all / the time for everybody," or engaging in frequent random sex. But it was only "like exercise." (A "story" is being narrated here in a tone and language that can be read by those outside of the gay community as humorously ironic remarks about the ambience of well-known cities on the east coast. But the "alternate" language of the poem sediments a "message" of sorts, meant for those who *are* members of the gay community. Such "coded" language probably would not have been used had O'Hara been writing in the 1980's.)

And the narrator goes on to explain that it means something different "to exercise" in Norfolk: "it means you've been to bed with a Nigra." The sex of the "Nigra" is not implied, and so the homosexual perspective of the poem remains sedimented within the text. Then we learn, "well it is exercise," but "it's better than Boston." The ambience of each city is facetiously "reported" here, and each city is linked with or compared to the one before. (And in this poem, unlike a great many in his canon, O'Hara makes use of connectives to emphasize the narrative voice.)

We are next "walking along the street / of Cincinnati"; not the *streets* "of Cincinnati," nor *a* street, nor "the street" *in* Cincinnati. These three choices of diction would mean *any* street in Cincinnati. O'Hara's word choice, "the street / of Cincinnati," gives "street" a special meaning; it was *the* street, one that was obviously known to be congenial to the gay community. And on "the street," the poet meets "Kenneth Koch's mother." Koch's "mother" was "fresh from the Istanbul Hilton"; she was a typical American tourist who, in a city like Istanbul, stayed at the Hilton. But she and the poet liked each other, and they "both liked Istanbul." (Given Istanbul's reputation for homosexual activity, we know why the poet/narrator might like that city, but there are, of course, a number of other reasons for each of them to like it.) In almost the exact center, or middle of this poem, O'Hara chooses a city in the American mid-west, introduces a middle-class mother/tourist, has the narrator meet her on "*the* [emphasis mine] street / of Cincinnati," and tells us that they like each other, and that they both like the exotic city of Istanbul. He unites opposites here in the center of the poem—"east" and "west," one continent and another, a member of the heterosexual community and one from the homosexual community—in another "disolve of time and geography," and the implication is that people of dissimilar persuasions can like each other, in spite of what happened in "Hackensack." On the other hand, this stanza, as well as the rest of the poem, can be read on the literal level as simply witty, chatty, sophisticated commentary.

But we are then taken from this idyllic situation to Waukegan, and meet a "furniture manufacturer." We are still in the midwest; however this experience is "horrible." It wipes out all "dreams of pleasantness from [his] mind"; both those of the remembrance of the pleasant meeting in Cincinnati, and of the "dream" of a pleasant sexual encounter in Waukegan. The experience is "like being pushed down hard / on a chair / [an obvious allusion to the *business* of the person whom he met, and to that person's sexual practices] it was like something horrible you hadn't expected," and that "is the most horrible thing." The narrator had expected something different here, and it was the "hard[ness]" and the unexpected brutality that was most "horrible."

Our fictive travelogue now takes us to Singapore and a "dreadful / disease." The "trivializing," "chatty" "voice" of the poem says it "was amusing to have bumps," but "they went into my veins / and rose to the surface like Vesuvius." The reality, of course, is that this experience cannot seriously be termed "amusing." "More often than not, O'Hara remains true to the gay attitudes of this period, minimizing saations [sic] of great pain and suffering with humor that neutralizes the seriousness of the harm done. . . ."[23] "Getting cured" compared with "learning to smoke" links its meaning with the "eruptions" of "Vesuvius," and also with the physical "eruptions" of adolescence, which is also usually the period during which one learns to smoke. But this also lightens, and so "codes," the serious content of these lines; that of the hazards of frequenting strange or unknown places.

The next stanza begins with a coordinating conjunction: "yet I always loved Baltimore," but the connection with Singapore is not made clear until the final line of the stanza, and then we find that it is a negative connection. O'Hara "corrects" himself in the second and third lines of this stanza, referring to "the porches which hurt your ass

/ no, they were the steps," and he then refers simultaneously to the custom, in Baltimore, of scrubbing the steps, and to the practice of anal sex, in the following line: "well you have a wet ass anyway." This tells us in another "coded" message why he likes Baltimore, even though he wishes "they'd stop scrubbing," and it points to the negative connection with Singapore, where they probably don't "scrub" enough.

We go from Baltimore's scrubbing to the ballet in San Francisco, still in the light "chatty," off-handed tone, where the narrator sees "the baby ballerina" who "looked like a cow." The reference to not knowing "the history of the ballet yet" becomes part of a deliberate ambiguity, in light of the final line of the stanza: "not that that taught me much." Whether the negative learning experience being referred to here is seeing "Toumanova," or later learning "the history of the ballet," is a moot question, but the asyndeton of this stanza does carry the idea that neither experience was fruitful.

In the penultimate stanza of the poem, however, there is a change of tone from the previous stanza, which was almost an aside from the mood of the poem itself. Here the tone changes from a rather dubious, somewhat negative one to one of alert expectancy. The first line begins with "now" used as an adverb, in the sense of "now hear this!" or perhaps simply as an attention-getting conversational introduction to what follows: "now if you feel like you want to deal with / Tokyo," and so refers to both the economic dealing that was beginning to take on importance in the '60s, and to the personal dealings of "handling" a sexual relationship in that teeming city. Comparing Tokyo to "Times Square at midnight" tells us that crowds of people are streaming in many directions at once, and also that a great deal of gay "cruising" is going on, and that while "you don't know where you're going / . . . you know." You know that whatever you are seeking you will find, and that you will indeed have "something to handle."

116

The final city on this fictitious journey is Harbin, a city in Manchuria. And *there* the narrator "knew / how to behave." That is, how to "behave" in the unfamiliar homosexual community of a foreign and remote country. Perhaps after his previous experience in Tokyo he was somewhat prepared, but that an occidental would know "how to behave" in Manchuria obviously serves notice that the poet is humorously stretching the limits of credibility. At the same time, he is also suggesting that members of an "oppressed minority" can *never* really "know how to behave." And, he suggests that they may have to go to "Harbin" in order to be free to be themselves. The words "it was glorious" refer both to knowing "how to behave" and to "that / was love sneaking up on me through the snow." The narrator "felt" it was "love" because of all the "postcards," "smiles," "kisses," and "grunts" (necessary means of communication, when the partners don't know each others' language), and he reiterates, "that was love but I kept on traveling." These examples of the "signs" of love are actually superficial symbols, and so the irony in the repetition of "that was love" is heightened by the final words of the poem, "but I kept on traveling." There is wry humor throughout this poem but there is a "bittersweet" quality to the humor in the final lines; under the best of circumstances, as well as under the most superficial, the poet/narrator, as a member of the gay community, must always be prepared to keep on "traveling." There is a community story buried in this poem, and the community benefits from the "hidden," or "coded," sedimented advice.[24]

In this section of the essay the focus has been on a number of poems in O'Hara's canon that re-creates his experiences, and his perceptions, of gay life in the ambience of the city in the 1950s and '60s. The poems discussed here are representative of a large segment of his canon that has been ignored because of its controversial content, or that has been "rewritten;" that is, has been read as poetry that is simply "camp," "chatty," or "trivial." O'Hara's gay language in these poems often does appear as simply enjoyable conversation—chatty and articulate—and it is sometimes superficial, usually non-moralistic, yet often ironic and sympathetic at the same time. His deliberate "trivial-izing," however, frequently has a sense of urgency, since gay language "is a trivialization that speaks and hides its catastrophe in relation to a future."[25]

In these poems, O'Hara addresses the concerns as well as the pleasures of the homosexual in the sophisticated urban environment of the city. So it seems fitting here to return to Whitman, the 19th Century American poet who shared many of the same concerns and pleasures (but who used a different "language" with which to encode them in his poetry), and who was much admired by O'Hara. Let us look once again at a poem discussed earlier, and see it here in a natural juxtaposition to Frank O'Hara's 20th century gay, urban poetic exploration of the "secret smile":

City of orgies, walks and joys,
City whom that I have lived and sung in your midst
        will one day make you illustrious,
Not the pageants of you, not your shifting tableaus,
        your spectacles, repay me,
Not the interminable rows of your houses, nor the ships
        at the wharves,
Nor the processions in the streets, nor the bright
        windows with goods in them,
Nor to converse with learn'd persons, or bear my share
        in the soiree or feast;
Not those, but as I pass O Manhattan, your frequent and
        swift flash of eyes offering me love,
Offering response to my own—these repay me,
Lovers, continual lovers, only repay me.
                        ("City of Orgies," *LofG*, p. 107)

CHAPTER V

CONCLUSION

This supplementary reading of Frank O'Hara's poetry has emphasized the importance of the recognition of his use of the language of the visual arts, and of his use of the layered language of homosexuality, to a more complete appreciation of the complexity of his poetic canon. His use of innovative subject matter, diction, and syntax, his ambivalence, his openness, results in a poetry of simultaneity and of spontaneity, one that re-creates the dynamics of a particular segment of life in New York City in the 1950s and early 1960s. And, as Benjamin DeMott says of William Dean Howells' *A Hazard of New Fortunes*, "*New Fortunes* is the first full revelation of the possibilities of New York as a literary subject . . . ,"[1] so we might also say of O'Hara's poetry that it is perhaps the first "revelation" of two seemingly unrelated aspects of New York City life— the aspects of art and of homosexuality—as a poetic subject.

The significance of O'Hara's poetic canon is enhanced by the reflection in much of his poetry of his knowledge and participation in the visual arts, and especially by his familiarity with the alternate, and hither-to all but ignored, contemporary gay life style that existed within the straight culture of New York City. As a poet, he said what he wanted to say about this previously shunned and ignored life-style, and he said it well. As Charles Altieri writes in his Preface to *Enlarging the Temple*, "I feel that critics have not yet fully appreciated the craft and intelligence of the poets studied herein. . . . The poets [Lowell, Bly, Olson, O'Hara, Snyder, Duncan, Creeley, Merwin, Levertov] share the decade's [1960s] general distrust of the values of Western humanism, but the alternatives they imagine are in my view more interesting as explorations of new sources of value and new definitions of the relationship between mind and world and clearly more typical of the ways of thinking that produced the decade's political turmoil and pursuit of alternative life-styles. . . . And unless we try to understand the characteristic styles and visions of this formative period in American poetry, I suspect that we will not fully appreciate the best work being written in the present."[2]

In a similar vein, René d'Harnancourt, then Director of the Museum of Modern Art, tells us: "Frank O'Hara, the poet, was part of the community of artists who are giving form to the issues, tensions, and release of our turbulent time and who, by doing so, are shaping the living fabric of the present. Frank O'Hara, the art critic and curator, was also part of that group who are called to use judgment and considerable action to make the artists' work accessible to all who may need it."[3]

The strategies O'Hara uses in giving form to, and in countering, his personal tensions and anxieties as well as those of our time, are manifold, as we have seen in the poems discussed in previous chapters. Like Whitman, O'Hara's poetic aspirations "are related to a constant theme in American poetry, the relation between the self and the world."[4] And, again like Whitman, that relationship was made more complex by his homosexual orientation. But unlike Whitman, O'Hara's poetic aspirations are expressed in and are more closely aligned with the genre of the lyric, rather than in an emphais on the creation of the epic. And in exploring the relation between himself and the world in his poetry, O'Hara re-creates that relationship through his constant awareness of the trivial and the mundane, simultaneously with his contemplation of the significant, and often, of the infinite. His emphasis is on the present moment as he is living it and he eschews the use of symbol just as he avoids verbal pomposity, since neither, for him, are part of the "present moment." O'Hara's directness of language is reflected upon in Robert Creeley's account of a conversation that Creeley had with Robert Duncan: "Speaking of Frank O'Hara, he notes that extraordinary poet's attempt to 'keep the *demand* on the language as *operative*, so that something was at issue all the time, and, at the same time, to make it almost like chatter on the telephone that nobody was going to pay attention to before . . . that the language gain what was assumed before to be its trivial uses. . . ."[5]

And so we find O'Hara to be a poet of ambivalence; he allows the reader to see the mind of the observer/constructor at work, and he expresses mixed feelings, without judgment, concerning his observations and experiences. There is nothing that is too crass or too sublime to be included, since his poetry is a re-creation of life as he perceived and experienced it. His ambivalence is most often expressed in a dialogue with himself (or with his "imaginary interlocutor"); two voices, one often correcting the other, one often naive and the other cynical.[6] The antinomy of depression and enthusiasm is seen as well in O'Hara's work, and it reflects the romantic idealism in his poetic, as well as his place in the continuity of the Romantic strain in American poetry.

O'Hara also expresses his ambivalence while expressing his modern-day tension by "correcting himself," or answering himself, or adjusting his perspective, immediately within the poem: "I am tired today but I am not / too tired. I am not tired at all. . . ." And, he often uses an escape into fantasy: "that angel seems to be leading the horse into Bergdorf's. . . ." Often, O'Hara speaks in the language of the visual arts to distance himself from the tensions of the moment.

> Well, I have my beautiful de Kooning
> to aspire to. I think it has an orange
> bed in it, more than the ear can hold.

And his use of the alternate language of the gay community allows him to express his ambivalence, his tension, and his release, in varying voices, as we have seen in, for example, "Homosexuality," "Song (Is it dirty,)" and "At the Old Place."

O'Hara's poetic "openness," commented on by John Ashbery and discussed above, his openness in the sense of the availability of his poetry and in the sense of that quality of American realism in his poetry—perceiving clearly and presenting honestly (even subject matter that can be expected to be shunned or avoided)—is a quality upon which the poet himself shall have the final word:

"My Heart"

> I'm not going to cry all the time
> nor shall I laugh all the time,
> I don't prefer one "strain" to another.
> I'd have the immediacy of a bad movie,
> not just a sleeper, but also the big,
> overproduced first-run kind. I want to be
> at least alive as the vulgar. And if
> some aficionado of my mess says "That's
> not like Frank!", all to the good! I
> don't wear brown and grey suits all the time,
> do I? No. I wear workshirts to the opera,
> often. I want my feet to be bare,
> I want my face to be shaven, and my heart—
> you can't plan on the heart, but
> the better part of it, my poetry, is open.
>
> (*CP*, p. 231. Written in 1955,
> published in 1970.)

NOTES

Chapter I

[1]Alexander Smith, Jr., *Frank O'Hara: A Comprehensive Bibliography*, (New York & London: Garland Publishing, Inc., 1980), pp. 201-230. (This section, titled "Writings Relating to Frank O'Hara," does not include articles listed in the *MLA International Bibliography*, and in a number of Digests and Indices, q.v. p. 202).

[2]Marjorie Perloff, *Frank O'Hara: A Poet Among Painters*, (New York: George Braziller, 1977), pp. 34 and 67.

[3]Alan Feldman, *Frank O'Hara*, (Boston: Twayne Publishers, 1979), pp. 114 and 135.

[4]Feldman, p. 157.

[5]Gerald Burns, "Portrait of the Artist as Charming," *Southwest Review*, (Spring 1974), p. 201.

[6]A. Poulin, Jr., ed., *Contemporary American Poetry*, (Boston: Houghton Mifflin Company, 1971), p. 379.

[7]Mutlu Konuk Blasing, "Frank O'Hara and the Poetics of Love," in *The Art of Life*, (Austin & London: University of Texas Press, 1977), p. 139.

[8]Irving Sandler, *The New York School: The Painters and Sculptors of the Fifties*, (New York: Harper & Row, 1978), p. 1.

[9]Helen Vendler, *Part of Nature, Part of Us*, (Cambridge: Harvard University Press, 1980), p. 180.

[10]Vendler, pp. 189-194.

[11]Donald Hall, "Donald Hall: An Interview By Liam Rector," *The American Poetry Review*, Jan/Feb 1989, p. 45.

124

[12]Susan Holohan, "Frank O'Hara's Poetry," in *American Poetry Since 1960,* (Great Britain: W. & J. Mackay Limited, 1973), pp. 114-116.

[13]James Schyler, "James Schyler: An Interview By Mark Hillringhouse," *The American Poetry Review,* March/April 1985, p. 5.

[14]Thomas Meyer, "Glistening Torsos, Sandwiches, and Cocacola," *Parnassus: Poetry in Review,* No. 6 (1977), p. 251.

[15]Anthony Libby, "O'Hara on the Silver Range," *Contemporary Literature,* No. 17 (1976), p. 241.

[16]Libby, p. 254.

[17]Charles Altieri, Enlarging the Temple: *New Directions in American Poetry During the 1960's,* (Lewisburg: Bucknell University Press, 1979), p. 238. The segment of this work that is devoted to O'Hara comes from an earlier essay by Altieri, "The Significance of Frank O'Hara," which was originally published in *Iowa Review,* 4, (1973). I am indebted to both the essay and the book cited here, throughout my essay).

[18]Altieri, p. 119.

[19]Paul Carroll, *The Poem In Its Skin,* (Chicago: Big Tank Publishing Co., 1968), pp. 154-168.

[20]Robert Penn Warren, "Impure Poetry," In *The Kenyon Critics,* John Crowe Ransom, ed., (Cleveland and New York: The World Publishing Company, 1951), p. 38.

[21]Carroll, pp. 157-163.

[22]Charles Molesworth, "The Clear Architecture of the Nerves: The Poetry of Frank O'Hara," *Iowa Review,* 6 (1974), 70-74.

[23]Kenneth Koch, "All the Imagination Can Hold," *The New Republic*, (January 1 and 8, 1972), pp. 23-25.

[24]Bill Berkson, ed. Afterword, *In Memory of My Feelings—A Selection of Poems by Frank O'Hara*, (New York: The Museum of Modern Art, 1967), p. 1.

[25]Donald Allen, ed., *The New American Poetry: 1945-1960*, (New York: Grove Press, Inc., 1960), p. xi.

[26]John Ashbery, Introduction, *The Collected Poems of Frank O'Hara*, Donald Allen, ed., (New York: Alfred A. Knopf, Inc., 1971), pp. vii-xi. (*The Collected Poems* will be subsequently cited as *CP* and is the definitive primary source used.)

[27]Cleanth Brooks, Jr., "Three Revolutions in Poetry, Part II, Wit and High Seriousness," *The Southern Review*, 1, No. 2 (1935), p. 328.

[28]Bruce Boone, "Gay Language as Political Praxis: The Poetry of Frank O'Hara," *Social Text*, 1 (Winter 1979), pp. 59-62. I find Boone's premises (of a repressed sexual content in O'Hara's poetry, and of the hidden use of the language of an "alternative" group) to be valid, and they will be discussed in subsequent pages.

[29]Although Ashbery worked in France for the Paris *Herald Tribune* from 1955 to 1965, he maintained a close connection and interaction with the other New York poets.

[30]Ron Padgett and David Shapiro, eds., Preface *Anthology of New York Poets*, (New York: Random House, 1970), p. xxx.

[31]Molesworth, p. 69.

[32]John Clellon Holmes, "Unscrewing the Locks: The Beat Poets," *Poets of the Cities: New York and San Francisco, 1950-1965*, (New York: E. P. Dutton & Co., Inc., 1974), p. 64.

[33]I find Myers' distinction between "The New York School of Poets," and "Poets of the New York School" neither clear nor useful in a discussion of the artistic qualities of this diverse group of poets, but his description of them, as quoted above, seems to me to be an accurate one.

[34]Robert M. Murdock, "Assemblage: Anything and Everything. Late 50's," in *Poets of the Cities: New York and San Francisco, 1950-1965,* (New York: E. P. Dutton & Co., Inc., 1974), p. 32.

[35]Kenneth Koch, "Poetry Chronicles," *Partisan Review,* 28 (1961), 130-132. Also cited in Perloff, *Poet Among Painters,* p. 69.

[36]Kenneth Koch, "Frank O'Hara and His Poetry: An Interview With Kenneth Koch," in *American Writing Today,* (Washington, D.C.: U. S. Internat. Communication Agency, 1982), pp. 249-263.

[37]Pastoral, here, is used in the sense of the term that defines "pastoral" as the poetry of a "city man longing for the country." *Princeton Encyclopedia of Poetry and Poetics,* (Princeton: Princeton University Press, 1972), p. 603.

[38]Raymond Williams, *The Country and the City,* (New York: Oxford University Press, 1973), pp. 148-240.

[39]Malcom Bradbury, "Cities of Modernism" in *Modernism: 1890-1930,* (New York: Penguin Books, 1978), pp. 96-101.

[40]Modernists such as Crane and Mayakovsky (unlike Eliot) explained the unreality of the "unreal" city as a failure of art, not as a human failure (q.v. Hyde, "The Poetry of the City," *Modernism: 1890-1930,* pp. 338-339).

[41]Altieri, p. 111.

[42]Hugh Kenner, *A Homemade World: The American Modernist Writers,* (New York: William Morrow and Company, Inc., 1975), p. 195.

[43]This was reprinted in *Audit*, and is included in the essay section of *Collected Poems*, pp. 498-499. There is also another "statement" (that was never sent) for the Paterson Society. This is not commented upon here because it registers O'Hara's point-of-view in only a negative sense, and therefore I do not consider a discussion of it to be productive in the light of my present purpose. It can be found in *Collected Poems*, pp. 510-511.

[44]Charles O. Hartman, *Free Verse: An Essay on Prosody*, (Princeton: Princeton University Press, 1980), p. 98.

[45]Altieri, pp. 18 and 113.

[46]As Richard Poirier describes it in *The Performing Self*, (New York: Oxford University Press, 1971), p. xiii, "performance" is "any self-discovering, self-watching, finally self-pleasuring response. . . ."

[47]Michael Davidson, "Languages of Post-Modernism," *Chicago Review*, 1 (Summer 1975), p. 12.

[48]Altieri, pp. 117-119.

[49]Myers, p. 20.

[50]O'Hara, "Personism," *CP*, p. 499.

[51]Henry M. Sayre, "David Antin and the Oral Poetics Movement," *Contemporary Literature*, 23 (Fall 1982), 428-450.

[52]Marjorie Perloff, in *The Poetics of Indeterminancy: Rimbaud to Cage*, (Princeton: Princeton University Press, 1981), places O'Hara in the line of poets of "indeterminancy"—poetry considered not as verse, but as "*language art* or 'word-system'" (pp. 43-44) and mentions him in connection with David Antin's talk poems. She says Antin's poems are examples of the "process of discovery; their stance, like John Ashbery's or Frank O'Hara's or Jackson MacLow's, is that of the *improvisatore*" (p. 151).

128

[53]Mutlu Konuk Blasing, *American Literature: The Rhetoric of Its Forms*, (New Haven: Yale University Press, 1987), p. 11.

[54]Boone, p. 71.

NOTES

Chapter II

[1]Perloff, pp. 86-96 (q.v. for commentary on O'Hara's art criticism).

[2]The last two lines of "A Step Away From Them," *CP*, p. 258.

[3]Libby, "O'Hara on the Silver Range," p. 240. O'Hara also collaborated with numerous visual artists in works that combined their art with his poetry. He collaborated with Larry Rivers, Grace Hartigan, Franz Kline, Norman Bluhm, Jasper Johns, Michael Goldberg, and others (q.v. Smith, pp. 165-179). An exhibition of many of these collaborations, *Art With the Touch of a Poet: Frank O'Hara*, was held at The Williams Benton Museum of Art, The University of Connecticut, Storrs, 1/24/83-3/13/83.

[4]Frank O'Hara, *Jackson Pollock*, (New York: George Braziller, Inc., 1959), p. 15.

[5]O'Hara, pp. 21-22.

[6]Marcel Brion et al., *Art Since 1945*, (New York: Washington Square Press, Inc., 1962), p. 268.

[7]Peter and Linda Murray, *A Dictionary of Art and Artists*, (Baltimore: Penguin Books, 1963), p. 3.

[8]Sam Hunter, *Modern American Painting and Sculpture*, (New York: Dell Publishing Co., Inc., 1963), pp. 150-152.

[9]Libby, p. 255.

[10]This was first published in O'Hara's monograph on Pollock, in 1959.

[11]q.v. "A Short Chronology," CP, p. xiv.

[12]Libby, pp. 256-257.

[13]O'Hara frequently refers to specific times and dates in his poetry; "The Day Lady Died" (*CP*, p. 325), one of his most well-known poems, begins "It is 12:30 in New York a Friday / three days after Bastille Day. . . ."

[14]Hunter, in *Art Since 1945*, p. 276.

[15]*CP*, p. 302.

[16]Eugene Goodheart, "Literature as a Game," *Tri Quarterly*, 52 (Fall 1981), p. 142.

[17]J. A. Cuddon, *A Dictionary of Literary Terms*, (Garden City: Doubleday & Co., 1977), p. 563.

[18]"To a Poet" was written in 1954. In a letter to Bill Berkson dated 8/12/62, with regard to his well known poem written in 1956, "Why I Am Not a Painter," O'Hara addresses Berkson's concern that he (O'Hara) put painting before poetry; in the letter, he calls poetry "the highest art" (q.v. Perloff, p. 18).

[19]q.v. "Personism," *CP*, p. 498.

[20]"[P]ublic," to O'Hara at the time, would most probably be the small coterie of poets and critics who were conversant with his poetry, many of whom met often at the San Remo, "the literary bar" (as O'Hara refers to it in his "Memoir," in *Larry Rivers*, the catalog for a Rivers exhibition at the Poses Institute of Fine Arts, Brandeis University, in 1965).

[21]This poem was first published "as a mimeographed pamphlet by Tibor de Nagy Gallery in 1953, on the occasion of an exhibition of Grace Hartigan's twelve paintings called *Oranges*, which incorporated the twelve pastorals." ("Notes on the Poems," CP, p. 519).

[22]"Notes on the Poems," *CP*, p. 540.

[23]Thomas Hess, *Willem de Kooning,* (New York: George Braziller, Inc., 1959), p. 22 (q.v. plate 49).

[24]Hunter, p. 284.

[25]Hess, *Willem de Kooning,* q.v. plates 111-138.

[26]Suzanne Ferguson, "Crossing the Delaware with Larry Rivers and Frank O'Hara: the post-modern hero at the Battle of Signifiers," in *Word Image: A Journal of Verbal/Visual Enquiry,* 2 (1) (1986): 27-32.

[27]Ferguson, p. 29.

[28]*CP*, pp. 233-34.

[29]Ferguson, p. 31.

[30]q.v. "Notes on the Poems," *CP*, p. 545.

[31]This is, however, an example of the language that has been called "light," "arty," and "trivial."

[32]q.v. "Personism," *CP*, p. 498.

[33]Walt Whitman, "When I Heard at the Close of Day," in *Walt Whitman: Leaves of Grass and Selected Prose.* (New York: Holt, Rinehart and Winston, Inc., 1949), pp. 104-105. This edition will subsequently be referred to as LofG, and is the definitive primary source used.

[34]The words, "the secrecy our smiles take on before people . . . ," epitomize the homosexual relationship of the '50s and '60s, and perhaps to some extent, even that of the '80s.

[35]The attribution to Rembrandt of *David and Saul, The Man With the Golden Helmet,* "and now even the *Polish Rider* in the Frick Collection . . ." is being questioned. "The *Polish Rider* is ascribed to the obscure Willem Drost. . . ." (See David Freedberg, "How Rembrandt

Made It," rev. of *Rembrandt's Enterprise*, by Svetlana Alpers, *The New York Review of Books*, 18 Jan. 1989, p. 29.

[36]The biographical references here and throughout the poem are apparent, but the poem works as well, as a paean to a lover, for the reader who is not aware of the facts of the O'Hara-Vincent Warren connection.

[37]Boone, p. 66.

NOTES

Chapter III

[1]Edmund Keeley, "The 'New' Poems of Cavafy," in *Modern Greek Writers*, (Princeton: Princeton University Press, 1972), pp. 133-134.

[2]Keeley, Biographical Note, in *C.P. Cavafy: Collected Poems*, (Princeton: Princeton University Press, 1980), pp. 250-251. (*C. P. Cavafy: Collected Poems* will subsequently be cited as *C.P.Cavafy* and is the definitive primary source used.)

[3]Michael Grant, *The Rise of the Greeks*, (New York: Macmillan Publishing Company, 1987), p. 180.

[4]Grant, p. 32.

[5]Karl Malkoff, "Varieties of Illusion in the Poetry of C. P. Cavafy," *Journal of Modern Greek Studies*, 5(1987): p. 23.

[6]George Economou, "Eros, Memory and Art," in *The American Poetry Review*, 10, No. 4, July/August 1981, pp. 30-31.

[7]W. H. Auden, "Introduction," *The Complete Poems of Cavafy*, by C. P. Cavafy, trans. Rae Dalven (New York: Harcourt Brace, 1961), p. ix.

[8]Keeley, "The 'New' Poems of Cavafy," pp. 133-34.

[9]Harold Aspiz, "The Spermatic Imagination," in *On Whitman: The Best from* American Literature, Edwin H. Cady & Louis J. Budd, eds., (Durham: Duke University Press, 1987, p. 289.

[10]Gay Wilson Allen, *The Solitary Singer*, (New York: Grove Press, 1955), p. 536.

134

[11]Joseph Cady, "Drum-Taps and Nineteenth Century Male Homosexual Literature," in *Walt Whitman Here and Now*, Joann P. Kreeg, ed. (New York: Greenwood Press, 1985), p. 52.

[12]Allen, p. 423.

[13]M. Jimmie Killingsworth, "Sentimentality and Homosexuality in Whitman's 'Calamus,'" in *ESQ: A Journal of the American Renaissance*, 29(1983), p. 145.

[14]Al Logan Slagle, Afterword, *The Good Red Road: Passages into Native America*, by Kenneth Lincoln with Al Logan Slagle (San Francisco: Harper & Row, 1987), p. 167.

[15]Floyd Stovall, "Main Drifts in Whitman's Poetry," in *On Whitman: The Best from* American Literature, (Durham: Duke University Press, 1987), pp. 9-10.

[16]Gregory Jusdanis, *The Poems of Cavafy: Textuality, Eroticism, History*, (Princeton: Princeton University Press, 1987), p. 99.

[17]Peter Bien, *Constantine Cavafy*, Columbia Essays on Modern Writers Pamphlet No. 5, (New York: Columbia University Press, 1964), p. 4.

[18]Alan Helms, "'Hints . . . Faint Clews and Indirections': Whitman's Homosexual Disguises," in *Walt Whitman: Here and Now*, Joann P. Krieg, ed., (Westport: Greenwood Press, 1985), p. 63.

NOTES

Chapter IV

[1]Edmund White, "The Political Vocabularly of Homosexuality," *The State of the Language,* (Berkeley and Los Angeles: University of California Press, 1980), pp. 244-245.

[2]In MS 535, "Music" has "Ilaria del Carreto [sic]" written below it (*CP*, p. 533). Loosely translated, this would mean "Aria of a Pushcart," and might be a free association with this lyric poem because the poem was conceived (and possibly written) while O'Hara was "pausing" for something to eat at an inexpensive, quick-service lunch counter.

[3]Eleanor Honig Skoller, "Franked Letters: Crossing the Bar," in *Visible Language*, No. 3, (1980), p. 307.

[4]q.v. Perloff, n. 41, p. 216.

[5]*CP*, p. 548.

[6]q.v. "Ode to Michael Goldberg ('s Birth and Other Births)," *CP*, p. 296. (According to the *O.E.D.*, Venus was first connected with venereal disease in 1591, in Catton's *Gemancie*.)

[7]"Notes on the Poems," *CP*, p. 531.

[8]Robert Martin, *The Homosexual Tradition*, (Texas: University of Texas Press, 1979), p. 165.

[9]White, p. 236.

[10]H. W. Janson, *History of Art*, (Englewood Cliffs: Prentice-Hall, Inc., 1969), pp. 512-513.

[11]We will see a more explicit example of this diction in "At the Old Place."

[12]q.v. Laud Humphreys, *Tea Room Trade*, (Chicago: Aldine Publishing Company, 1975).

[13]It is interesting to note that as complex, and rich, and revealing a poem as "Homosexuality" is, it was not included in O'Hara's *Selected Poems*. The explicitness of its title may have been the cause of its exclusion, or perhaps it simply did not fit into the "structure" that Donald Allen refers to in his short editorial comment in *The Selected Poems of Frank O'Hara*.

[14]In one sense, O'Hara actually presents himself as a "conservative" in this poem. He decries the "whorish" aspect of his own community, just as a conservative in the straight group would tend to do concerning the same aspect of his or her own community.

[15]This poem, like "Homosexuality," does not appear in *Selected Poems*. It is another revealing poem, for the time in which it was written, in terms of both the gay life style, and of specific participants.

[16]Susan Sontag, "Notes on Camp," in *Partisan Review*, 31, (Fall 1964), pp. 515-530.

[17]Since the poem was written in 1955, the tone of relief and freedom at being able to be "themselves" is not one of exaggerated playfulness, but a re-creation of the reality of the moment.

[18]Perloff, p. 113.

[19]This poem was written in 1961, and in "Notes on the Poems," *CP*, p. 551, we are told that an earlier title, "Dear Vincent," was crossed out. "Vincent Warren had given FOH the autobiography of Mary Desti, Isadora Duncan's great friend." The title of the poem can also be a humorous reference to Stevenson's *Travels with a Donkey*, since the poem is surely one with "picaresque" qualities.

[20]White, p. 246.

[21]Two of Richard Wagner's grandsons were connected with Bayreuth during O'Hara's lifetime, but because of the fictive and humorous tone of the poem, it should no doubt be assumed that O'Hara's reference to "the Wagners" is non-specific.

[22]The connection was through V.W., whose name was part of the original title of the poem.

[23]Boone, p. 74.

[24]Boone, p. 83.

[25]Boone, pp. 81-82.

NOTES

Chapter V

[1]Benjamin DeMott, Afterward, *A Hazard of New Fortunes* by William Dean Howells, (New York: New American Library, Inc., 1965), p. 434.

[2]Altieri, p. 9.

[3]René d'Harnoncourt, Preface, *In Memory of My Feelings—A Selection of Poems by Frank O'Hara*, Bill Berkson, ed., (New York: The Museum of Modern Art, 1967).

[4]Roger Asselineau, "Walt Whitman," in *Eight American Authors*, James Woodress, ed., (New York: W. W. Norton & Co., Inc., 1971), p. 254. Asselineau here is commenting on Roy Harvey Pearce's statement in *The Continuity of American Poetry*.

[5]Robert Creeley, "On the Road: Notes on Artists and Poets 1950-1965," in *Poets of the Cities and San Francisco 1950-1965*, Catalog for exhibition organized by the Dallas Museum of Fine Arts and Southern Methodist University, (New York: Dutton, 1974), p. 58.

[6]I have incorporated here ideas expressed in conversation, by Alexander Smith, Jr., concerning O'Hara as a poet of ambivalence.

BIBLIOGRAPHY

Primary Sources

Art With the Touch of a Poet: Frank O'Hara (unbound exhibition catalog). The William Benton Museum of Art. Storrs: The University of Connecticut, 1983.

Cavafy, C.P., *C.P. Cavafy: Collected Poems.* Trans. Edmund Keeley and Phillip Sherrard. Ed. George Savidis. Princeton: Princeton University Press, 1980.

O'Hara, Frank. "Collected Proses, An Answer." *Semi-Colon,* 11, no. 1 (1955) 2-3.

_____. *Frank O'Hara: Early Writing.* Ed. Donald Allen. Bolinas: Grey Fox Press, 1977.

_____. *Frank O'Hara: Poems Retrieved.* Ed. Donald Allen. Bolinas: Grey Fox Press, 1977.

_____. *Jackson Pollock.* New York: George Braziller, Inc., 1959.

_____. "Larry Rivers: A Memoir." In *Larry Rivers* (exhibition catalog). Waltham: Poses Institute of Fine Arts, Brandeis University, 1965.

_____. "O the Dangers of Daily Living." In *The Poet's Story.* Ed. Howard Moss. New York: Simon and Schuster, 1973.

_____. "Personism: A Manifesto." In *The Collected Poems of Frank O'Hara,* Ed. Donald Allen. New York: Alfred A. Knopf, Inc., 1971.

_____. *The Collected Poems of Frank O'Hara.* Ed. Donald Allen. New York: Alfred A. Knopf, 1971.

_____. *The Selected Poems of Frank O'Hara.* Ed. Donald Allen. New York: Alfred A. Knopf, 1974.

142

Whitman, Walt. *Walt Whitman: Leaves of Grass and Selected Prose.*
Ed. and Introd. Sculley Bradley. New York: Holt, Rinehart and
Winston, Inc., 1949.

Secondary Sources

Allen, Donald, ed. *The New American Poetry: 1945-1960.* New York:
Grove Press, Inc., 1960.

_____ and Warren Tallman, eds. *The Poetics of the New American
Poetry.* New York: Grove Press, Inc., 1973.

_____, ed. *Standing Still and Walking in New York.* Bolinas: Grey

Fox Press, 1975.

Allen, Gay Wilson. *The Solitary Singer.* New York: Grove Press, 1955.

Altieri, Charles. *Enlarging the Temple: New Directions in American
Poetry During the 1960's.* Lewisburg: Bucknell University Press,
1979.

_____. "Presence and Reference in a Literary Text: The Example
of Williams' 'This is Just to Say.'" *Critical Inquiry,* 5, no. 3, (Spring
1979), 489-510.

_____. "The Significance of Frank O'Hara." *Iowa Review,* 4 (1973),
90-104.

Antin, David. "and ive called this talk tuning." *Alcheringa,* 3, no. 2
(1977), 92-125.

_____. "Modernism and Postmodernism: Approaching the Pres-
ent in American Poetry." *boundary 2,* 1, no. 1 (1972), 98-133.

Ashbery, John. Introd. *The Collected Poems of Frank O'Hara*. Ed. Donald Allen. New York: Alfred A. Knopf, Inc., 1971.

Aspiz, Harold. "The Spermatic Imagination." In *On Whitman: The Best from* American Literature. Eds. Edwin H. Cady and Louis J. Budd. Durham: Duke University Press, 1987.

Asselineau, Roger. "Walt Whitman." In *Eight American Authors*. Ed. James Woodress. New York: W. W. Norton & Co., Inc., 1971.

Auden, W. H. "The Poet and the City." In *The Dyer's Hand and Other Essays*. New York: Vintage Books, 1962.

_____. Intro. *The Complete Poems of Cavafy*. Trans. Rae Dalven. New York: Harcourt, 1961.

Barnstone, Willis, et al., eds. *Modern European Poetry*. New York: Bantam Books, 1978.

Barthes, Roland. *The Pleasure of the Text*. Trans. Richard Miller. New York: Farrar, Straus and Giroux, Inc., 1975.

Baudelaire, Charles-Pierre. *Poesies Choisies*. Notices by Andre Ferran. Paris: Librairie Hachette, 1936.

Benamou, Michel. "Presence and Play." In *Performance in Postmodern Culture*. Eds. Michel Benamou and Charles Caramello. Madison: Coda Press, Inc., 1977.

Berkson, Bill, ed. In *Memory of My Feelings—A Selection of Poems by Frank O'Hara*. New York: The Museum of Modern Art, 1967.

_____. "Frank O'Hara and His Poems." *Art and Literature*, 12 (Spring 1967), 53-63.

Bien, Peter. *Constantine Cavafy*. Columbia Essays on Modern Writers Pamphlet No. 5. New York: Columbia University Press, 1964.

Blasing, Mutlu Konuk. *American Poetry: The Rhetoric of its Forms.* New Haven: Yale University Press, 1987.

_____. "Frank O'Hara and the Poetics of Love." In *The Art of Life.* Austin: University of Texas, 1977.

Blasing, M. K. "Frank O'Hara's Poetics of Speech, the Example of 'Biotherm.'" *Contemporary Literature,* 23 (82), 52-64.

Bloom, Harold. "The Glory and the Sorrows of American Romanticism." In *Romanticism: Vistas, Incidences,* Continuities. Eds. David Thorburn and Geoffrey Hartman. Ithaca: Cornell University Press, 1973.

Boone, Bruce. "Gay Language as Political Praxis: The Poetry of Frank O'Hara." *Social Text,* 1 (Winter 1979), 59-92.

Bradbury, Malcolm. "The Cities of Modernism." In *Modernism: 1890-1930.* Eds. Malcolm Bradbury and James McFarlane. New York: Penguin Books, 1978.

_____ and James McFarlane. "The Name and Nature of Modernism." In *Modernism: 1890-1930.* Eds. Malcolm Bradbury and James McFarlane. New York: Penguin Books, 1978.

Brion, Marcel, et al. *Art Since 1945.* New York: Washington Square Press, Inc., 1961.

Brooks, Cleanth, Jr. "Three Revolutions in Poetry, Part I, Metaphor and the Tradition." *The Southern Review,* 1, no. 1 (July 1935), 151-163.

_____. "Three Revolutions in Poetry, Part II, Wit and High Seriousness." *The Southern Review,* 1, no. 2 (Autumn 1935) 328-338.

Brown, Frederick. "Creation versus Literature: Breton and the Surrealist Movement." In *Modern French Criticism*. Ed. John K. Simon. Chicago: The University of Chicago Press, 1972.

Butterick, George. "Frank O'Hara." In *American Poets Since World War II, Part 2*. Ed. Donald J. Greiner. Gale's Dictionary of Literary Biography Series. Detroit: Gale Research Company, 1980.

Bunge, Nancy. "William Stafford: An Interview By Nancy Bunge." *The American Poetry Review*, 10, no. 6 (1981), 8-11.

Burns, Gerald. "Portrait of the Artist as Charming." *Southwest Review*, (Spring 1974), p. 201.

Cady, Joseph. "'Drum Taps' and Nineteenth Century Male Homosexual Literature." In *Walt Whitman: Here and Now*. Ed. Joann P. Krieg. Westport: Greenwood Press, 1985.

Caramello, Charles. "On Styles of Postmodern Writing." In *Performance in Postmodern Culture*. Eds. Michel Benamou and Charles Caramello. Madison: Coda Press, Inc., 1977.

Carroll, Paul. "An Impure Poem About July 17, 1959." In *The Poem in the Skin*. Chicago: Big Tank Publishing Co., 1968.

Crasnow, Ellman. "Poems and Fictions: Stevens, Rilke, Valéry." In *Modernism: 1890-1930*. New York: Penguin Books, 1978.

Creeley, Robert. "On the Road: Notes on Artists and Poets 1950-1965." In *Poets of the Cities and San Francisco 1950-1965* (catalog for exhibition organized by the Dallas Museum of Fine Arts and Southern Methodist University). New York: Dutton, 1974.

Davidson, Michael. "Languages of Post-Modernism." *Chicago Review*, 1 (Summer 1975), 11-22.

DeMott, Benjamin. Afterword. *A Hazard of New Fortunes*. By William Dean Howells. New York: New American Library, 1965.

D'Harnoncourt, René. Preface. *In Memory of My Feelings.* Ed. Bill Berkson. New York: The Museum of Modern Art, 1967.

Economou, George. "Eros, Memory and Art." *The American Poetry Review,* (July/Aug 1981), 30-31.

Ellmann, Richard, and Charles Feidelson, Jr., eds. *The Modern Tradition: Backgrounds of Modern Literature.* New York: Oxford University Press, 1965.

Federman, Raymond. "Federman: Voices Within Voices." In *Performance in Postmodern Culture.* Eds. Michel Benamou and Charles Caramello. Madison: Coda Press, Inc., 1977.

Feldman, Alan. *Frank O'Hara.* Boston: Twayne Publishers, 1979.

Ferguson, Suzanne. "Crossing the Delaware With Larry Rivers and Frank O'Hara: the post-modern hero at the Battle of Signifiers." *Word Image: A Journal of Verbal/Visual Enquiry.* Vol. 2 no. 1 (1986), 27-32.

Freud, Sigmund. *Leonardo Da Vinci: A Study in Psychosexuality.* Trans. A. A. Brill. New York: Vintage Books, 1947.

Freedberg, David. "How Rembrandt Made It." Rev. of *Rembrandt's Enterprise* by Svetlana Alpers. *The New York Review of Books,* (18 Jan 1989), 29-31.

Frye, Northop. *The Great Code: The Bible and Literature.* New York: Harcourt Brace Jovanovich, Inc., 1981.

Fussell, Paul. *Poetic Meter and Poetic Form.* New York: Random House, 1979.

Goodheart, Eugene. "Literature as a Game." *Tri Quarterly,* 52 (Fall 1981), 134-149.

Guillory, Daniel L. "Leaving the Atocha Station: Contemporary Poetry and Technology." *Tri Quarterly*, 52, (Fall 1981), 165-181.

Grant, Michael. *The Rise of the Greeks*. New York: Macmillan Publishing Company, 1980.

Hall, Donald, ed. *Contemporary American Poetry*. Baltimore: Penguin, 1962.

_____. "Donald Hall: An Interview By Liam Rector." *The American Poetry Review*, (Jan/Feb 1989), 39-46.

Hartman, Charles O. *Free Verse: An Essay on Prosody*. Princeton: Princeton University Press, 1980.

Helms, Alan. "'Hints . . . Faint Clews and Indirections': Walt Whitman's Homosexual Disguise." In *Walt Whitman: Here and Now*. Ed. Joann P. Krieg. Westport: Greenwood Press, 1985.

Hess, Thomas B. *DeKooning*. New York: M. Knoedler & Co., Inc., 1969.

Herbert. Robert L., ed. *Modern Artists on Art: Ten Unabridged Essays*. Englewood Cliffs: Prentice-Hall, Inc., 1964.

Holahan, Susan. "Frank O'Hara's Poetry." In *American Poetry Since 1960*. Great Britain: W. & D. Mackay Limited, 1973.

Holland, Norman N. *Poems in Persons*. New York: W. W. Norton & Co., Inc., 1973.

Holmes, John Clellon. "Unscrewing the Locks: The Beat Poets." In *Poets of the Cities: New York and San Francisco, 1950-1965* (catalog for exhibition organized by the Dallas Museum of Fine Arts and Southern Methodist University). New York: E. P. Dutton & Co., Inc., 1974.

Hough, Graham. "The Modernist Lyric." In *Modernism: 1890-1930*. Eds. Malcolm Bradbury and James McFarlane. New York: Penguin Books, 1978.

Howard, Richard. "Frank O'Hara." In *Alone With America*. New York: Atheneum, 1969.

Humphreys, Laud. *Tea Room Trade*. Chicago: Aldine Publishing Company, 1975.

Hunter, Sam. "The United States." In *Art Since 1945*. New York: Harry N. Abrams, Inc., Washington Square Press, 1962.

_____. *Modern American Painting and Sculpture*. New York: Dell Publishing Co., Inc., 1963.

Hyde, G. M. "The Poetry of the City." In *Modernism: 1890-1930*. Eds. Malcolm Brabury and James McFarlane. New York: Penguin Books, 1978.

Jaffé, H. L. C. *Twentieth Century Painting*. New York: The Viking Press, 1963.

Janson, H. W. *History of Art*. Englewood Cliffs: Prentice-Hall, Inc., 1969.

Jusdanis, Gregory. *The Poetics of Cavafy: Textuality, Eroticism, History*. Princeton: Princeton University Press, 1987.

Kazin, Alfred. *Contemporaries*. Boston: Little, Brown and Company, 1962.

Keeley, Edmund. "The New Poems of Cavafy." In *Modern Greek Writers*. Eds. Edmund Keeley and Peter Bien. Princeton: Princeton University Press, 1972.

Kenner, Hugh. *A Homemade World: The American Modernist Writers*. New York: William Morrow and Company, Inc., 1975.

Killingsworth, M. Jimmie. "Sentimentality and Homosexuality in Whitman's 'Calamus.'" *ESQ: A Journal of the American Renaissance,* 29 (1983), 144-153.

Koch, Kenneth. "All the Imagination Can Hold." *The New Republic.* (January 1 and 8, 1972), pp. 23-25.

_____. "A Note on Frank O'Hara in the Early Fifties." *Audit Poetry.* 4, no. 1 (1964), 32-33.

_____. "Frank O'Hara and His Poetry: An Interview With Kenneth Koch." In *American Writing Today.* Washington, D.C.: U.S. International Communications Agency, Vol 1 (1982), 249-263.

_____. "Poetry Chronicles." *Partisan Review,* 28 (January/ February 1961), 130-32, 134-36.

_____. *Rose Where Did You Get That Red?: Teaching Great Poetry to Children.* New York: Random House, 1973.

LeSueur, Joseph. "Four Apartments." In *Another World.* Anne Waldman. Indianapolis: The Bobbs-Merrill Company, Inc., 1971.

Libby, Anthony. "O'Hara on the Silver Range." *Contemporary Literature,* no. 17 (1976), 240-262.

Lincoln, Kenneth with Al Logan Slagle. *The Good Red Road: Passages into Native America.* San Francisco: Harper & Row, Publishers, 1987.

Lowry, Bates. *The Visual Experience.* New York: Harry N. Abrams, Inc., 1963.

Machlis, Joseph. *The Enjoyment of Music.* New York: W. W. Norton & Co., Inc., 1963.

Malkoff, Karl. "Varieties of Illusion in the Poetry of C. P. Cavafy." *Journal of Modern Greek Studies,* 5 (1987), 191-203.

150

Martin, Robert. *The Homosexual Tradition.* Austin: University of
Texas Press, 1979.

Meyer, Thomas. "Glistening Torsos, Sandwiches, and Coca-cola."
Parnassus: Poetry in Review, 6 (1977), 241-257.

Miller, James E., Jr. *A Critical Guide to* Leaves of Grass. Chicago:
University of Chicago Press, 1970.

Molesworth, Charles. "The Clear Architecture of the Nerves: The Poetry
of Frank O'Hara." *Iowa Review,* 6, iii-iv (1974), 61-74.

Moramarco, Fred. "John Ashbery and Frank O'Hara: The Painterly
Poets." *Journal of Modern Literature,* 5:3 (Sept. 1976), 436-463.

Moss, Howard, ed. *The Poet's Story.* New York: Simon and Shuster,
1973.

Murdock, Robert M. "Assemblage: Anything and Everything. Late
50s." In *Poets of the Cities: New York and San Francisco, 1950-
1965* (exhibition catalogue, organized by the Dallas Museum of
Fine Arts and Southern Methodist University). New York: E. P.
Dutton & Co., Inc., 1974.

Murray, Peter and Linda. *A Dictionary of Art and Artists.* Baltimore:
Penguin Books, 1963.

Myers, John Bernard, ed. *The Poets of the New York School.* Philadelphia: University of Pennsylvania, 1969.

Neumeyer, Alfred. *The Search for Meaning in Modern Art.* Englewood
Cliffs: Prentice-Hall, Inc., 1964.

Newman, Earnest. *Stories of the Great Operas.* Philadelphia: The
Blakiston Company, 1945.

Newmeyer, Sarah. *Enjoying Modern Art.* New York: Reinhold Publishing Co., 1963.

Nowottny, Winifred. *The Language Poets Use.* London: The Athlone Press, 1962.

Olson, Charles. "Projective Verse." In *The New American Poetry.* Ed. Donald Allen. New York: Grove Press, 1960.

Padgett, Ron, and David Shapiro, eds. *Anthology of New York Poets.* New York: Random House, 1970.

Paz, Octavio. *Children of the Mire.* Trans. Rachel Phillips. Cambridge: Harvard University Press, 1974.

Perloff, Marjorie. *Frank O'Hara: A Poet Among Painters.* New York: George Braziller, 1977.

_____. "From Image to Action: The Return of Story in Postmodern Poetry." *Contemporary Poetry,* 23 (Fall 1982), 411-427.

_____. *The Poetics of Indeterminancy: Rimbaud to Cage.* Princeton: Princeton University Press, 1981.

Poirier, Richard. *The Performing Self.* New York: Oxford University Press, 1971.

_____. *A World Elsewhere: The Place of Style in American Literature.* New York: Oxford University Press, 1966.

Poulin, A., Jr., ed. *Contemporary American Poetry.* Boston: Houghton Mifflin Company, 1971.

Ransom, John Crowe, ed. *The Kenyon Critics.* Cleveland and New York: The World Publishing Company, 1951.

Read, Herbert. *The Meaning of Art.* Baltimore: Penguin Books, 1964.

Rosenblum, Robert. *Modern Painting and the Northern Romantic Tradition: Friedrich to Rothko.* New York: Harper & Row, Publishers, Inc., 1975.

152

Rothenberg, Jerome. "New Models, New Visions: Some Notes Toward." In *Performance in Postmodern Culture*. Eds. Michel Benamou and Charles Caramello. Madison: Coda Press, Inc., 1977.

Sandler, Irving. *The New York School: The Painters and Sculptors of the Fifties*. New York: Harper & Row, 1978.

Sayre, Henry M. "David Antin and the Oral Poetics Movement." *Contemporary Literature*, 23 (Fall 1982), 428-450.

Schechner, Richard. "The Crash of Performative Circumstances: A Modernist Discourse on Postmodernism." *Tri Quarterly*, 52 (Fall 1981), 85-103.

Schuyler, James. "James Schuyler: An Interview By Mark Hill-ringhouse." *The American Poetry Review*, March/April 1985, 5-12.

Shapcott, Thomas. "Two Tombstones." *Poetry* (April 1973), pp. 41-47.

Shaw, Robert B., ed. *American Poetry Since 1960*. Great Britain: W. & J. Mackay Limited, 1973.

Short, Robert. "Dada and Surrealism." In *Modernism: 1890-1930*. Eds. Malcolm Bradbury and James McFarlane. New York: Penguin Books, 1978.

Skoller, Eleanor Honig. "Franked Letters: Crossing the Bar." *Visible Language*, 14, no. 3 (1980), 306-319.

Smith, Alexander, Jr. *Frank O'Hara: A Comprehensive Bibliography*. New York: Garland Publishing, Inc., 1980.

Smith, Eunice Clark and John K. Savocool, eds. *Voix du Siecle*. New York: Harcourt, Brace & World, Inc., 1960.

Sontag, Susan. "Notes on Camp." *Partisan Review*, 31 (Fall 1964), 515-530.

Stambolian, George, and Elaine Marks, eds. *Homosexualities and French Literature: Cultural Contexts/Critical Texts.* Ithaca: Cornell University Press, 1979.

Stovall, Floyd. "Main Drifts in Whitman's Poetry." In *On Whitman: The Best from* American Literature. Durham: Duke University Press, 1987, 1-19.

Tate, Allen. "Is Literary Criticism Possible?" In *The Man of Letters in the Modern World.* New York: Meridian Books, 1955.

_____. "Tension in Poetry." In *The Man of Letters in the Modern World.* New York: Meridian Books, 1955.

Vendler, Helen. *Part of Nature, Part of Us.* Cambridge: Harvard University Press, 1980.

_____. "The Virtues of the Alterable." *Parnassus,* 1, i (1972), 5-20.

Viereck, Peter. "Strict Form in Poetry: Would Jacob Wrestle with a Flabby Angel?" *Critical Inquiry,* 5, no. 2 (1978), 203-223.

Warren, Robert Penn. "Impure Poetry." In *The Kenyon Critics.* Ed. John Crowe Ransom. Cleveland and New York: The World Publishing Company, 1951.

Wellek, Rene and Austin Warren. *Theory of Literature.* 3rd ed. New York: Harcourt, Brace & World, Inc., 1970.

White, Edmund. "The Political Vocabulary of Homosexuality." In *The State of the Language.* Ed. Leonard Michaels and Christopher Ricks. Berkeley and Los Angeles: University of California Press, 1980.

Williams, Raymond. *The Country and the City.* New York: Oxford University Press, 1973.

Williams, William Carlos. *The Selected Poems of William Carlos Williams.* Introd. Randall Jarrell. New York: New Directions Publishing Corporation, 1966.

Wolfflin, Heinrich. *Principles of Art History.* New York: Dover Publications, Inc., 1950.

INDEX OF TITLES